Refire! Don't Retire

Make The Rest Of Your Life The Best Of Your Life

Ken Blanchard
Morton Shaevitz

Copyright Page from the Original Book

Refire! Don't Retire

BK

Berrett-Koehler Publishers, Inc.
1333 Broadway, Suite 1000
Oakland, CA 94612-1921
Tel: (510) 817-2277, Fax: (510) 817-2278
www.bkconnection.com

Ordering information for print editions
Quantity sales. Special discounts are available on quantity purchases by corporations, associations, and others. For details, contact the "Special Sales Department" at the Berrett-Koehler address above.
Individual sales. Berrett-Koehler publications are available through most bookstores. They can also be ordered directly from Berrett-Koehler: Tel: (800) 929-2929; Fax: (802) 864-7626; www.bkconnection.com
Orders for college textbook/course adoption use. Please contact Berrett-Koehler: Tel: (800) 929-2929; Fax: (802) 864-7626.
Orders by U.S. trade bookstores and wholesalers. Please contact Ingram Publisher Services, Tel: (800) 509-4887; Fax: (800) 838-1149; E-mail: customer.service@ingrampublisherservices.com; or visit www.ingrampublisherservices.com/Ordering for details about electronic ordering.

First Edition
Hardcover print edition ISBN 978-1-62656-333-9
PDF e-book ISBN 978-1-62656-334-6
IDPF e-book ISBN 978-1-62656-335-3

2014-1

Production Management: Michael Bass Associates

Cover Design: Irene Morris

TABLE OF CONTENTS

More Praise for Refire! Don't Retire

"This book is full of simple truths of profound value to mature adults in transition who are ready to focus on significance rather than success. It is also playfully inspiring, encouraging the reader to be open and spontaneous through such things as identifying a 'Last Minute Gang' and living by the 'Nothing Ordinary' rule. It's a delightful read!"

—Mary Lindenstein Walshok, Professor of Sociology and Dean, University Extension, University of California, San Diego

"Companies could help their executives before leaving by using this book. C-level executives are often at a loss after stepping out of a power seat. This book would've made my transition much easier as I floundered to regain my purpose and passion. I will use *Refire!* lessons to help my leaders move from success to significance and regain the passion they once had for running their organization."

—Alan Sorkin, Executive coach, Vistage International

"Ken Blanchard is a master storyteller. Morton Shaevitz has been working for years in the arena of older adults and looks at aging from a new and different perspective. *Refire! Don't Retire* goes down easy and is packed with practical wisdom."

—Bob Buford, founder, Leadership Network and The Halftime Institute and author of *Halftime* and *Drucker & Me*

"Refire your love, joy, passion, purposefulness, success, and significance with this magnificent book! Drink deeply of the wisdom of Ken and Morton's brilliance so you can have a delightfully ageless future with ever more fun."

—Mark Victor Hansen, cocreator of the Chicken Soup for the Soul series and author of The Miracles in You series

"*Refire!* is a blueprint for a new, exciting, vibrant, meaningful, serving life. If you have to have a tattoo, this title would make a good one. Ten thousand people turn sixty-five every day. They should all be required to read this book."

—Hyrum Smith, author of *The Power of Perception* and *What Matters Most*

"*Refire! Don't Retire* will re-energize you and your relationships—as well as your book club!"

—Iris F. Litt, MD, Professor Emerita of Pediatrics and former Director, Center for Advanced Study in the Behavioral Sciences, Stanford University

To "Zig" Ziglar

1926–2012

An author, salesman, motivational speaker, and inspiring friend who first introduced Ken to the concept of refiring. With his incredible, positive energy, Zig made a difference in the lives of everyone with whom he came in contact.

Introduction

It's often said that there is no such thing as a coincidence. Given the dynamic nature of the universe, when things happen, they happen for a reason. So, when the two of us met on an early morning flight from San Diego to New York, it was not by chance.

Perhaps it was *serendipity*—something that was destined to happen, that was meant to be. If we pursue this concept further, we find the Yiddish word *bashert,* which roughly translates into "a happy, joyous event that was meant for good."

"So what are you into and what's new in your life?" was the beginning of our plane conversation. For the next fifteen minutes, we spoke with growing enthusiasm and animation. We talked about the things we were doing, and especially what we were excited about. When Morton mentioned he was working in the area of older adults and looking at aging from a new and different perspective, Ken piped up and said he'd been thinking about similar issues. The term he was using was *refire*—an attitude of embracing the years ahead with enthusiasm rather than apathy. At that moment, this book was born.

We continued talking nonstop, leaning over the airline seats that separated us. Finally, we had to be forcibly seated by the flight attendants so that the plane could take off. Throughout the five-hour flight to New York, we continued to exchange ideas until the movie came on and silenced us. As we deplaned, we decided to meet soon to continue the conversation.

By the time we met again, Morton had attended a birthday party for someone he had known in college. He came back intrigued by what he had observed. It wasn't just that everyone looked older—of course they did. It was how differently they were approaching aging. While some seemed intellectually energetic and engaged in the world, others seemed to have little joy or sense of a future—nothing they were striving for.

Coincidentally, Ken and his wife Margie had just returned from a two-week cruise. Ken reported similar observations about his fellow travelers, most of whom were seniors. Some were vivacious, taking advantage of the classes and activities offered by the cruise ship, while others were withdrawn and didn't come alive until mealtime.

As we discussed what each of us had experienced, we began wondering what accounted for these two different ways our age group was handling aging. Why were some people seeing the rest of their lives as an opportunity, while others were treating it as some kind of sentence?

Talking about this with our adult children, we discovered that this view of life was not limited to seniors—our middle-aged kids had some friends who also had the "best years are behind us" approach to life.

We thought about those of our friends and colleagues who were embracing—rather than enduring—life and tried to figure out what made them different. We concluded that much depended on what they believed about growing older and how they were approaching life. We also concluded that if those who were merely enduring could be helped to think differently, they might begin to behave differently and, if you will, *refire.*

What are you going to do with the rest of your life to make it healthy, joyful, and meaningful? We wrote *Refire* as a guide to answering that question. In the parable and suggestions that follow, we hope you find inspiration to create an exciting future.

1

A Wake-up Call

Larry Sparks took his wife's hand as they headed to the entrance of the hotel ballroom. He did so partly for moral support, but mostly because after nearly forty years of marriage, he was prouder than ever of Janice, his still beautiful bride.

"The registration table's got to be up here somewhere," he said.

Around them a crowd of people—nearly all of them approximately their age—moved with Larry and Janice toward the ballroom doors.

Larry leaned over and whispered into Janice's ear. "Who are all these old geezers?" he joked.

She looked over at him and smiled. "I'm sure they're thinking the exact same thing about us."

"Nah," said Larry. At that moment the registration table came into view beneath a sign that read:

LINCOLN HIGH SCHOOL

45TH REUNION—GO EAGLES!

Janice ducked into the ladies' room and Larry was busy filling out a name tag when he heard a vaguely familiar voice behind him.

"Larry Sparks! Is that you?"

Larry turned to see what he thought was a complete stranger making his way toward him. The man appeared world weary, with slumped shoulders and thinning gray hair. It wasn't until the man gave Larry a good-natured slap on the back that he recognized Rob Briggs, the smart kid who'd helped him through chemistry and physics in his junior and senior years.

"Hey, Rob. Wow. Long time no see! How you been?"

"Ah, you know, not great—but consider the alternative, right?" Rob let out a half-hearted laugh. "I wasn't sure if it was you or Kevin. But I knew it had to be one of you guys."

With those words, Larry had a major flashback. This was just like high school, all right. During his entire four years at Lincoln, Larry was forever being mistaken for his fraternal twin, Kevin.

"I'm afraid Kevin couldn't make it," said Larry. "He's off somewhere putting together another deal." Larry shook his head. The sibling rivalry he'd once felt with Kevin had mellowed. Still, he couldn't help but compare himself to his twin.

"So Kevin's still an overachiever, huh?" Rob laughed. "I guess things don't change that much in forty-five years. Are you still with Janice?"

"Absolutely, and we're having more fun than ever."

Right on cue, Janice appeared at Larry's side. She recognized Rob at once and gave him a big hug. The three of them caught up on kids and careers and promised to reconnect during the big dinner and dancing event at the end of the weekend.

***

Two nights and a lot of reminiscing later, Larry and Janice returned to the hotel ballroom and enjoyed a surprisingly good reunion dinner. After a chocolate mousse dessert, the music began. Janice—the extrovert of the pair—dragged Larry onto the dance floor for a few numbers and then encouraged him to join her in finding and catching up with old friends.

They were heading back to their table when they finally found Rob again.

"You two having fun?" Rob asked.

"We're having a blast with a lot of folks," said Janice, "but I'm worried about a few people in this crowd."

"What do you mean?" asked Rob.

"Based on our observations over the course of this weekend, the biggest activity for some of our fellow classmates is eating," Larry replied.

"And eating a lot," Janice added. "Not to mention drinking."

Rob shrugged. "Isn't that what you're supposed to do at a reunion?"

Larry nodded toward the dance floor. "Yeah, but they're missing out on the dancing, and only a few people have turned out for the outdoor activities that have been happening the past couple of days. I at least try to stay in shape. As I always say to Janice, 'Someday I want to be one of the four guys on the tour bus in Hawaii.'"

"The tour bus in Hawaii?" said Rob, looking puzzled.

Larry laughed. "Yeah. Whenever you see a crowd of seniors getting off a tour bus in Hawaii, there are about thirty well-preserved women and only about four old guys—because all the other men have died off."

They all had a good laugh at that.

"Kidding aside," said Janice, "it makes me sad that some of our fellow Eagles are approaching getting older as a life sentence rather than a wonderful opportunity."

"It's not just seniors who act that way," said Rob. "I work with a bunch of thirty- and forty-year-olds at a tech firm. You'd be shocked how many of these people do nothing after work but go home to their couches, complaining about old athletic injuries and mumbling jokes like, 'Old age is no place for sissies.'"

"That's a funny line, but it's a terrible motto," said Janice. "I want to embrace what's left of life, not complain about it."

Larry, an avid golfer, nodded and said, "I know I'm on the back nine, but I want to finish strong."

"If you want to finish strong, that's the person you should talk to," said Rob. He pointed to a handsome man with a thick head of salt-and-pepper gray hair who was chatting with some others near the dance floor.

"Is that our ninth-grade biology teacher, Mr. Jeffrey?" asked Larry.

"Yeah," said Rob, "but it's *Dr.* Jeffrey now. He taught for a couple of years but left teaching to go to graduate school and get his PhD. He now heads the department of psychology at our local university and teaches in the interdisciplinary psychology/philosophy program. He's become pretty well known. Really, you should go talk to him."

***

Larry tapped Dr. Jeffrey on the shoulder.

"Excuse me, sir. You were my favorite science teacher." He extended his hand. "Larry Sparks—and this is my wife, Janice."

"Good to see you, Larry!" said Dr. Jeffrey, vigorously shaking Larry's hand. "And hello, Janice."

"Biology wasn't exactly my best subject," said Larry. "Thanks for the B on that final. I know you were being kind."

"I'm sure you earned it," Dr. Jeffrey said with a laugh.

"I have to say, you look great," said Larry. "What are you up to these days? Are you retired?"

"I'm not even considering it!" bellowed Dr. Jeffrey. "Some of the greatest people in my field made their best contributions in their later years. I'm not retiring—I'm refiring!"

"*Refiring?* That sounds intriguing," said Janice. "What does it mean?"

Dr. Jeffrey didn't hesitate in answering. "To refire is to approach life with gusto. It's to see each day as an opportunity for adventure and learning! It's to infuse passion and zest into every area of your life—emotional, intellectual, physical, and spiritual. Heart, head, body, and soul." He punctuated each word with the very passion of which he spoke.

"Sounds like you've given this some serious thought," said Janice.

Dr. Jeffrey nodded. "I've spent the better part of the past decade studying aging and exploring how the later decades in life can be rewarding and dynamic rather than limited and depressing. I teach and write extensively on the subject. I'll be happy to give you guys some coaching if you ever feel yourself falling into a rut."

Before Larry or Janice could answer, a woman in a red dress grabbed Dr. Jeffrey by the sleeve and pulled him onto the dance floor.

***

All the way home, Larry and Janice compared notes on the reunion. Once again they talked about how sad it was that some of their classmates seemed resigned to declining health, limited activities, stale relationships, and dreams turning to dust.

"Do you think we're in a rut?"

Janice's question took Larry aback.

"No. Why?"

"You don't exactly seem as excited about your construction business as you used to be. And I know

I'm not approaching my life with gusto and infusing it with—what did Dr. Jeffrey call it?—passion and zest."

"Yeah, but come on," said Larry, suddenly feeling defensive as he pulled into the garage. "Is that even realistic? I mean, to a certain extent, life really is a grind."

"Now that's a zesty attitude, right there," kidded Janice as she got out of the car.

Inside the house, the phone was ringing.

"I'll get it," said Larry. He raced into the kitchen and caught it on the final ring.

"Hello?"

The line was silent. Larry thought he'd missed the caller and was about to hang up when he heard the distinct sound of a woman crying.

"Hello? Who is this?"

"It's Angie."

Angie—his brother's wife. Beneath her snuffling, her voice was very small.

"Are you okay, Ang?"

"He's gone, Larry." She sobbed openly now.

A cold wave of fear flowed through Larry's body. "What? Who's gone?"

"Your brother had a massive heart attack. He's gone, Larry! Our Kevin is gone."

2

A Visit with Dr. Jeffrey

Over the next several months, Kevin's death had a major impact on Larry. While he'd loved his brother with all his heart, he had always been concerned that Kevin was missing out on life because he was working all the time. Kevin's career had taken its toll not only on his health but also on his relationships—Angie was his third wife. Kevin had three kids from prior marriages. Reconnecting with them at the funeral, Larry realized they hadn't known their father very well. Kevin had always talked about the great things he planned to do someday, when things slowed down. Now that day would never come.

"I'm seriously thinking about stepping back from the business, Janice."

Janice looked up from packing her briefcase. "That's ironic. Here I am getting ready to interview to be the director of Learning Is for Everyone and you're planning on cutting back."

For the past five years, Janice had been a committed volunteer at Learning Is for Everyone, an organization that brought college students together with underprivileged kids for tutoring.

"The timing doesn't sound ideal," said Larry. "This means you're not going to be around nearly as much."

Janice said, "I know this isn't perfect timing for you, but the job's not going to be full-time. And when this opportunity came up, I thought about Kevin's death and I started to wonder, 'What am I waiting for?' Remember, your old teacher Dr. Jeffrey encouraged us to refire and add some zest to our lives, right?"

"But as I recall, refiring wasn't just about working. Jeffrey mentioned relationships, learning, and other things, too. Kevin's death has really got me thinking how much time I'm spending working. So I know I want to refire, but I'm not sure what that will look like for me."

Janice closed her briefcase and put it aside. "Dr. Jeffrey offered to give us coaching about refiring. This seems like the perfect time to take him up on that offer, since we're both searching for what's ahead—for each of us personally, as well as for us as a couple."

"Let's go see him!" said Larry.

***

As Larry and Janice pulled into the university parking lot for their appointment with Dr. Jeffrey, their first problem was finding a place to park.

"Now I see why they say a university consists of thousands of people gathered together around a common parking problem," Larry joked.

"That certainly seems to be true today, doesn't it?" said Janice. "I remember reading about Clark Kerr's final speech when he stepped down years ago as president of the University of California. He said he wished he'd known at the beginning of his tenure what he knew then—namely, the three goals of a university: First, winning football for the alumni. Second, sex for the students. And third, parking for the faculty."

"That's a good one," said Larry with a laugh.

After finally finding a spot, they walked to Dr. Jeffrey's building, where they sat in a pleasant waiting room until the receptionist called their names and ushered them to his office.

Dr. Jeffrey stood to greet them. "Come on in," he said.

"We appreciate your kind offer to give us some refiring coaching," said Larry.

"This works out for me too, because telling me about your experience will help me in my research," Dr. Jeffrey replied.

"Speaking of research," said Janice, "what are you finding in your studies that could help us in our refiring journey?"

"First," said Dr. Jeffrey, "it's become clear to me that a lot of people who have experienced outer success in their lives have inner turmoil. They are not lovers of themselves. We've found conclusive evidence that achievements and accumulation of wealth do not make people happy. Happiness is an inside-out job."

"I'd like to hear more about that," said Larry.

"When you're externally motivated around your achievements and popularity with others, somehow that doesn't result in inner peace. Your focus is on success, which plays out in accumulation of wealth, recognition, and power/status. While there's nothing wrong with accumulating wealth, receiving recognition for your efforts, and having some power and status, what's wrong is when you think that's who you are. When that's the case, you have to keep on getting more of each of those."

"Interesting," said Larry. "What's the answer to that?"

"There's plenty of emphasis on success in our culture. I'm finding we have to help people focus on significance as well."

"What's the difference?" asked Janice.

"Significance focuses on three different measures: generosity, service, and loving relationships.

"Generosity is the opposite of accumulating wealth. It involves giving your time, your talent, and your treasure to others," Dr. Jeffrey continued.

"That makes sense," said Larry. "I've always thought that making money for money's sake wasn't very valuable, but it has given me the opportunity to help others."

"Remember," said Dr. Jeffrey, "in our later years it's not only money we can share but also our wisdom, our time, and our talent.

"That leads to the second aspect of significance: service, which is the opposite of recognition. Now the focus is on helping others, not yourself. A pastor friend of mine put it well when he said that real joy in life comes when you get in the act of forgetfulness about yourself."

"And that happens when you are doing something kind for someone else," said Janice.

"That's true," said Dr. Jeffrey. "That leads to the third aspect of significance, which is loving relationships—the opposite of power/status. A friend of mine, John Ortberg, wrote a wonderful book called *When the Game Is Over, It All Goes Back in the Box.* It's a story about him and his grandmother. When he was young, she was an incredible Monopoly player. At the end of the game, she had everything and John had nothing. She would get this grin on her face and say, 'John, someday you're going to learn how to play the game.'"

Dr. Jeffrey continued, "One summer when John was about thirteen, a kid moved next door who was an ace Monopoly player. John practiced with him every single day, because he knew his grandmother was coming in September. When that day arrived, John ran to greet her and said, 'Hi, Grandma! How about a Monopoly game?'

"His grandmother's eyes lit up and she said, 'Let's go, John.' But John was ready for her this time. He came out of the chute and wiped his grandmother out. He said it was the greatest day of his life! His grandmother smiled and said, 'John, now that you know how to play the game, let me teach you a lesson about life: it all goes back in the box.'

"'What do you mean?' John asked. She said, 'Everything you accumulated—all the hotels, houses, utilities, cash—it all goes back in the box.'

"And how true that is," said Dr. Jeffrey with a smile. "You can accumulate all the money, recognition, and power/status you want in life, but at the end it all goes back in the box. The only thing you get to keep is your soul, and that's where you store who you loved and who loved you."

"That reminds me of the ending of the movie *Ghost,*" said Janice. "It ties right into that."

"I think I saw that a number of years ago," said Dr. Jeffrey.

"Yes, it's been around for a while. It's the story about a young financier, played by Patrick Swayze, who was killed by a supposed friend. He gets to stay on earth as a ghost to protect his girlfriend Molly, played by Demi Moore. And he gets to talk to her through the help of a clairvoyant by the name of Oda May, played by Whoopie Goldberg. At the end of the film, Sam has avenged his death and he, Molly, and Oda May are on the rooftop of Molly's apartment building. A white light starts coming toward them. Oda May says, 'They're coming for you, Sam.' Sam turns and looks at Molly. When he was alive, he never told Molly he loved her. She would say, 'Sam, I love you' and he would say, 'Ditto.' Now, with tears coming down his face, he says, 'Molly, I love you. I've always loved you.' And with tears in her eyes she says, 'Ditto.' Sam turns toward the light, then stops and turns to Molly one last time. 'Molly,' he says, 'the remarkable thing about this is that you can take the love with you.'"

"Wow," said Larry, "and that's the only thing we're going to take out of this world, isn't it?"

"I believe so," said Dr. Jeffrey.

"Wait a minute," said Janice. "This gets to what Larry and I were talking about this morning. He's thinking about cutting back on his work to focus on significance. But I feel like I've been focusing on significance for years, raising the kids and volunteering my time. I'd like to try a little success at this point in my life."

She turned to Larry. "And wouldn't you get a kick out of being introduced as the spouse of the director of Learning Is for Everyone?"

Larry laughed. "It may take me a few days to get used to it."

"Success and significance are not necessarily in conflict—and they don't have to happen in that order," said Dr. Jeffrey. "Wanting to experience a bit of success doesn't mean you've abandoned significance.

"The key," he continued, "is to make sure you are solid emotionally, intellectually, physically, and spiritually—or as I mentioned to you at the reunion, in the heart, the head, the body, and the soul. When those four are integrated, you become whole and create a powerful foundation for moving forward in your life. It establishes a framework for being a wise, loving, mature, creative, and balanced person."

"Sounds a little complicated," said Larry.

"Establishing that balance is not something that happens overnight," Dr. Jeffrey replied. "When I work with people on this, I tell them to anticipate at least a yearlong learning curve, focusing on each area for at least three months."

"Where should we start?" asked Larry.

"Let's start with your hearts—the emotional side. That's where our relationships come into play. But rather than me explaining the importance of emotional balance, I'd like for you to go see some friends of mine, Wendy and Harold Tong. They're a terrific couple who have just backed off from very active careers. They understand well the emotional side of life, and

I think they could give you a good handle on how relationships can really enhance this stage of your journey. My assistant will give you their contact information. Please go see them. After you've had a chance to think about and apply what you learn from them, let's get back together in about three months or so."

"Sounds good," said Larry as he smiled at Janice. "And thanks for helping us get started on our journey to refire."

PAUSE, REFLECT, TAKE ACTION

• Considering the emotional, intellectual, physical, and spiritual parts of your life, which one is getting the least attention—and how can you change that?

• What are you doing out of habit rather than zeal?

• What is the current balance between your striving for success and achieving significance?

• What can you do to be of service to others?

• Choose one service-oriented activity you can commit to doing now.

The First Key

Refiring Emotionally

3

Love Is the Key

The sun was breaking through the morning clouds when Janice and Larry arrived at the Tongs' house. Wendy and Harold greeted them at the door and welcomed them inside.

"Dr. Jeffrey told us you're interested in talking about refiring," Wendy said as she showed them to the living room. "That term took us aback, because we've been through a major refiring—literally."

"What do you mean?" asked Janice.

"Our original home was burned down in the wildfires that devastated this area a few years ago," said Harold. "Talk about refiring. We had to refire from the ground up."

"That must have been awful. What did you do?" asked Larry.

"We rented a home nearby and were planning to rebuild," Harold replied. "But our daughter-in-law was walking her dog in the neighborhood one morning and discovered that this house—which we'd always admired—had a for-sale sign on the lawn. We were able to buy it—and save the time and expense of rebuilding—so our house 'refiring' has a happy ending."

"But I'm sure you didn't come over to hear all about us," Wendy said as Janice and Larry settled onto the Tongs' comfortable sofa. "Dr. Jeffrey said he thought we might be able to help you refire emotionally."

"If you could make it through your house burning down, you obviously know a thing or two about emotional resilience," said Janice.

"I suppose we do," said Harold.

"Emotional health is certainly something we've worked on over the years," said Wendy. "It's especially important in relationships. We try to stay emotionally engaged in our relationships with family and friends, as well as with each other."

"Dr. Jeffrey said that having loving relationships was a big part of what he called 'moving from success to significance,'" said Janice. "Tell us about how you've refired emotionally with family and friends."

"A while ago," began Harold, "we noticed that sometimes we were being a little judgmental. If a friend did something that offended us, we tended to write them off. We realized that if we kept that up, pretty soon we'd be out of friends! Then I remembered something my mother told me when I was young. She said, 'There's a pearl of good in everyone if you search for it.'"

"That's beautiful," said Larry. "What a great way to look at others."

"We thought so," said Wendy, "so we started searching for the pearls. We began loving people even when they were engaging in unlovable behavior."

"That doesn't sound all that easy to do," said Janice.

"It wasn't, the first couple of times," said Wendy. "Then Harold and I realized we'd had plenty of practice with our kids! How many kids are loveable all the time?"

"Nobody's kids that I know," admitted Janice.

"But have you ever heard of anyone sitting their kids down and saying, 'This just isn't working out. We have to split up'?"

Larry laughed and said, "Good point. Even if the parents are divorced and hate each other, they continue to love their children."

"But aren't there some people whose pearl is so buried that they're not healthy to be around?" asked Janice.

Wendy nodded. "Sure. But we've found that's the exception rather than the rule."

"Tell us about how you've refired your relationship with each other," said Larry.

"We started paying attention to our feelings," said Wendy. "We noticed we had positive emotions and negative emotions. We consciously started placing more attention on the positive feelings."

"They key is recognizing which are which," said Harold. "To us, positive feelings are like love in action."

"That's an interesting way to put it," said Larry, "but I'm not sure I know what you mean. Could you tell us more about that?"

"Of course," said Harold. "I'm sure you've been to a lot of weddings."

"We have indeed," said Janice.

"You've undoubtedly heard the love passage from the Bible," continued Harold.

"You mean the one that goes, 'Love is patient, love is kind'?" asked Larry.

"Exactly," said Harold. "It comes from I Corinthians 13. Whether you're religious or not, it includes a wonderful list of positive feelings and the resulting love-based behaviors. In fact, I know it by heart." Harold recited:

Love is patient, love is kind.
It does not envy, it does not boast.
It is not proud.
It is not rude, it is not self-seeking.
It is not easily angered; it keeps no record of wrongs.
Love does not delight in evil
But rejoices with the truth.
It always protects, always trusts, always perseveres.

"I've always loved hearing that at weddings," said Janice.

Wendy said, "It is beautiful, isn't it? Harold and I talk about that passage periodically and ask ourselves if we're living by it. When we recite it out loud, it helps us take a look at our feelings. Right away we know which ones we need to be working on."

"It occurs to me," said Larry, "that the opposite of those positive feelings are negative emotions—like frustration, impatience, or even anger."

"That's right," said Harold. "Take that positive statement that love 'is not easily angered.' Having a bad temper is the one thing that can get us off of a loving track faster than anything else."

"How do you control that, if anger is a problem for you?" wondered Janice.

"First you have to recognize it as a problem," said Wendy. "Isn't that right, Harold?"

"Absolutely," said Harold. "Everyone has negative feelings at times, and while we may not be able to control how we feel, we are responsible for how we react to those feelings. Whenever I feel anger building, I try to stop and take a deep breath. If I can, I might go for a short walk to calm down—because I know if I let that anger out, it's not going to help the situation or make the world a better place."

"I think all of us would like to make the world a better place," said Larry.

Harold nodded. "Let me ask you: do you have a plan for how you're going to do that?"

Larry and Janice laughed. "I guess we don't," Janice said with a smile.

"Yet we can all make the world a better place through the moment-to-moment decisions we make as we interact with the people we come in contact with at home, at work, and in the community," said Harold.

"You're not talking about one day at a time—you're talking about one moment at a time," said Larry.

"That's right," said Harold. "Suppose, as you leave your house in the morning, your spouse yells at you and it upsets you. What do you do? You have a choice: you can yell back, or you can go back in the house, ask what's upsetting them, hug them, and wish them a good day. If someone cuts you off on the way to work, you have a choice: will you chase that person down and make an obscene gesture, or will you take a deep breath and hope they don't hurt themselves or somebody else? We have choices all the time about how we deal with others."

"That's true," said Janice. "I forget that sometimes."

"It's never too late to understand that we have choices," said Wendy. "For example, sometimes we get into ruts, not only with each other but also with our friends. We need to become more spontaneous and ready to go. Doing the same things the same way with the same people doesn't contribute to your emotional health or anyone else's."

"I read an interesting story about that recently," said Larry. "This man realized he didn't know most of his neighbors very well. Everybody just drove in and out of their garages—they rarely talked to each other or spent time together. He wanted to change that. He remembered that when he was a kid, he and his friends had some of their best times at sleepovers. So he decided to go out on a limb. He sent a note to all his neighbors that said:

> *Most of us don't know each other very well, but I'd like to change that. How about getting together next Saturday for a summer potluck? I have a big backyard with a fire pit. So come over, play some badminton, and hang out! If any of you want to make a mini-vacation of it, bring your toothbrush and let's make it a sleepover! I have an empty guestroom that sleeps two, plus a sofa bed. All you need to do is bring your favorite food. Don't forget the marshmallows!*

"I'll bet most of his neighbors thought the sleepover part was a little weird—maybe even a little risky," said Harold.

"Most of them probably did," said Larry. "Quite a few neighbors came for the potluck, had a great time, and went home that evening. But one of his neighbors took the invitation to heart and came prepared for a sleepover. This neighbor was an older gentleman who lived close by. The host had known him casually for some time. They talked throughout the evening, watched each other's favorite television shows, and even roasted some marshmallows over the fire. Finally, the two neighbors retired to separate rooms for a good night's sleep. In the morning they had breakfast together, went for a walk, and parted good friends.

"The older gentleman spread the word to all his neighbors about what a meaningful time the sleepover had been. Pretty soon walks, dinners, movies, and even sleepovers became a common practice. The neighborhood became a real neighborhood."

"What fun!" said Wendy. "That story perfectly highlights the importance of being flexible and open to new experiences. As I said earlier, without flexibility you can get in a rut. You can't enrich your current relationships or forge new ones if you keep on doing the same things in the same ways."

"What I hear you suggesting," said Janice, "is that we need to become engaged with others."

"That's right," said Harold. "We can't keep growing emotionally if we isolate ourselves from others. Wendy and I believe that feedback is the breakfast of champions. If you really get to know others well, you'll grow close enough that they'll be willing to praise you when you're fun to hang around with and give you honest feedback when you're being obnoxious or a stick in the mud."

"So our suggestion for the emotional aspect of your journey to refire," said Wendy, "is to get to really know each other, as well as the people around you. Be willing to take interpersonal risks and learn from them."

"We really appreciate your insights and suggestions," said Larry.

"Yes, thank you," said Janice. "Larry and I will see what we can do to grow emotionally with each other as well as with the people around us."

With that, Larry and Janice gave their new friends a hug and headed home.

PAUSE, REFLECT, TAKE ACTION

- What might you do to reach out to someone close to you—a spouse or good friend—to revitalize that relationship?
- What new people can you reach out to and make a part of your life?
- What can you do to let others know you care about them?
- What is your plan for making the world a better place?

• Tell a person you care about that you appreciate them.

4

Building Relationships

It didn't take long for Larry and Janice to begin applying what they had learned from Wendy and Harold. In fact, it started happening the next day.

"Who was that on the phone?" asked Janice.

"Oh, it was Rob."

Janice frowned. "Again? Seems like we've been seeing an awful lot of him since the reunion. What did he want?"

"Come on, Janice. I know Rob's not the best listener, but remember what Wendy and Harold told us about looking for the pearl of good in everyone."

"Yeah, but anytime I say anything to Rob, he hijacks the conversation and makes it about him."

Larry smiled. "Yeah, but do you know a more generous guy than Rob?"

"You're right—we've had some wonderful times with him. So what did he want?"

He asked if we wanted to go see a movie with him tonight."

"Tonight?" Janice questioned.

"Yeah, tonight, and he wants to go in about a half hour. But the movie's playing at the Cinema Guild, and we'd have to meet him in twenty minutes," Larry explained. "I really hate the Cinema Guild."

"So what did you say?" asked Janice.

"I said no, because there isn't enough time and the movie isn't something I'm interested—"

"Well, what's the movie?" Janice interrupted.

"It's some type of a cartoon," said Larry.

"You mean an animated movie?"

"Yeah, a cartoon."

"No, animated movies are not cartoons. They're a new kind of media that you're not very comfortable with."

"It's not that I'm not comfortable with it—I'd just rather watch real people."

"You may want to rethink that," said Janice. "Now *why* did you say no?"

"Because like I told you, there's not enough time and it's at the Cinema Guild—a theater I don't like—and it's the kind of movie I'm not sure I want to see."

"Honey, if you listen to what you just said, it sounds kind of stuffy and maybe even a little bit rigid. Remember what Wendy and Harold taught us yesterday about being flexible."

"Me? Stuffy and rigid?" said Larry with a smile.

"Yeah, you!"

"What are you talking about?" Larry joked.

"We haven't seen a movie in several weeks. So if Rob invites us to one, why not go?"

"But we haven't even had dinner yet."

"So what? We can skip dinner, or even have popcorn for dinner."

"Popcorn for dinner!"

"Yes. Popcorn for dinner."

"That just sounds weird."

"Maybe it's weird to you, but it sounds like fun to me. Would it be more fun to stay at home, cook dinner, eat, and do nothing for the rest of the night? Come on, Larry. Let's give it a try! I'm going to call Rob back right now and tell him we'll meet him. What do we have to lose?"

Larry reluctantly agreed, mumbling that he still thought it sounded pretty weird.

Within twenty minutes, Larry and Janice were running up to the box office, where Rob had just arrived.

"Okay, let's do it!" said Janice.

As they walked in, Larry was still grumbling, but Janice was having great fun.

"How about a hot dog?" Janice suggested.

"A hot dog?"

"Yeah, how about a hot dog? We haven't had dinner yet; let's have a hot dog, a soda, and a cookie for dessert!"

"A hot dog, soda, and a cookie for dessert. There goes our healthy eating plan."

"Yep. I don't think this one time of eating junk food is going to hurt us. Doing something different and spontaneous will be fun."

After the movie, Rob, Janice, and Larry engaged in a lively conversation as they walked toward the exit.

"What a terrific movie!" said Larry.

"Yes," said Rob. "I'd read the reviews and thought I'd like it."

"And if Rob likes something, he assumes everybody will like it," said Janice with a laugh.

"In this case Rob was right," said Larry. "I did like it—even though it was a cartoon!"

"An animated movie," Rob and Janice chimed in.

"Okay, okay, okay. An animated movie."

The three went into a café to get some coffee and continued talking about the movie. Rob said he had been planning to spend the evening at home until he picked up the paper and saw the movie's positive reviews.

"I thought of calling you guys," said Rob, "but the past few times when I've called at the last minute, you seemed to get offended. I was almost going to pass. I wasn't surprised when you said no, Larry, but was really happy when Janice called back and said yes."

With that, Larry and Janice told Rob about their discussions with Dr. Jeffrey and their commitment to refiring their relationships—looking for the positive and being more spontaneous.

"Good for you two," said Rob. "I'm glad you started refiring with me. And doing things at the last minute is not such a bad idea. That we have busy lives is just a fact of life, but when good things pop up unexpectedly, we should jump at the chance to say yes."

"But the way I like to go to the movies is first to go out to dinner, then see the movie, and then have a chance to talk afterward," Larry said.

"Yeah, but it doesn't always have to be that way," said Rob. "Did you have fun tonight? Do you wish you'd stayed home? Are you sorry you're sitting here with us instead of watching TV at home? Sometimes doing things at the last minute is fun."

As the conversation continued, Larry thought, *I guess Harold and Wendy were right. Not only am I having a good time with Rob, but he's even encouraging me to practice what they preached.*

***

The following week Janice came home excited. "Larry, I got the director's job!" she announced. "Why don't we celebrate by having Phil and Kelly over for dinner?"

Larry and Janice had known Phil and Kelly for more than two decades. Phil was a retired accountant and Kelly had been a fourth grade teacher at the local elementary school until a few years ago, when she began doing pottery and entering her work in local art shows.

"That's a good idea," said Larry. "We haven't seen them for a long time. When should we have them for dinner?"

"Well, how about tonight?" said Janice.

"Tonight?"

"Yeah, tonight!"

"But it's already six o'clock. They probably have plans," said Larry.

"Well, maybe they don't."

"But even if they don't have plans, how are we going to get a dinner together in an hour?" he asked.

"Let's go get some of that great take-out from the Thai restaurant."

"Take-out?"

"Yeah, take-out," said Janice.

"But I like it when we cook a really nice meal for our friends," Larry countered.

Janice smiled. "Are you being rigid again?" she kidded. "Are you forgetting what a good time we had with Rob last week?"

"Okay," said Larry. "I'll give it a try again."

Janice put the phone on speaker and dialed Phil and Kelly's number. When Kelly picked up, Janice asked, "Hey, what are you guys doing for dinner?"

On the other end of the line, Kelly said, "We haven't thought about it yet."

"Why don't you come over here for some take-out Thai food?"

"When?" asked Kelly.

"How about in an hour?"

"In about an hour?"

"Yeah!"

"Well—hold on."

There was a pause and Janice and Larry could hear Kelly consulting with Phil. Suddenly Kelly was back on the line.

"Okay!" she said.

At dinner that night, Larry and Janice talked with Phil and Kelly about what had happened. They shared about their meeting with Wendy and Harold and described their experience the week before, going to the movies with Rob at the last minute.

At that point, Larry stood up and announced, "Okay! I am declaring us charter members of the Last-Minute Gang!"

"The Last-Minute Gang?" asked Janice.

"Yes, the Last-Minute Gang! And I'm going to call Rob and tell him he's a charter member, too."

After that, they all got excited about the Last-Minute Gang. They admitted that they had fallen into the rut of doing the same things, the same way, with the same people. After a while, they began to form Last-Minute Gangs with their other friends.

When asked what the Last-Minute Gang was all about, Larry would explain that being a member of the gang meant you felt free to ask anybody to do anything at the last minute. The person who answered the call had the right to say yes or no, but unless they had a compelling reason not to say yes—for example, they were already eating when you invited them for dinner or were already at the movies when you invited them to a play—they said yes.

Larry summed it up this way:

"Unless there's a legitimate reason to say no, you say yes!"

Larry's willingness to be open to new experiences was soon tested.

***

"So how did it go?" Janice asked as Larry came walking in the door.

"Incredible," said Larry.

"Really?" said Janice. "I'm surprised. What made it incredible?"

Larry had just come back from dinner at a sushi restaurant with his fifteen-year-old grandson, Paul. Larry had been reluctant to go, thinking, *How can you have a whole meal of raw fish?* But Paul had prodded him and Janice had urged him to go.

"So, what happened?" asked Janice.

"First, it took me a half hour to find the place, because it was in the back of a shopping mall, and you know how I am with directions," said Larry.

"Of course I know how you are with directions. The GPS has saved your life."

"You're right. When I finally found the restaurant, it was like a diner, with a long counter and three or four tables. I arrived first, so I sat at the counter and watched the people come in. In a few minutes, every single seat was taken. Everyone kept looking at the chefs, who were cutting and sorting and putting things on plates, then giving them to people. When I got a menu, the only thing I could order was something to drink, so I got a beer for myself and a soda for Paul.

"At that point a server came over and asked me if it was my first time at a sushi place. I admitted it was and asked her how it worked.

"She smiled and said, 'We keep bringing you food until you tell us to stop.'

"'Really?' I said. I didn't ask how much it cost, because Paul had already told me, 'It's going to be *really* expensive, Grandpa.'

"A few minutes later, Paul arrived and gave me a hug. I was drinking my beer, he began drinking his soda, and one of the chefs behind the counter came over and said, 'Ready?'

"And Paul said, 'You bet!'

"So for the next hour, they served us sushi. Every dish was different, and every time, the chef told us whether to put a sauce on it and what sauce to use."

"And?" asked Janice.

"And it was great—the food just kept coming and coming. Paul showed me a new way to use chopsticks and how to put the sauces on. He was so funny and friendly that he had everyone in the restaurant smiling.

"We finally were stuffed," continued Larry, "so I paid the bill and we headed out of the restaurant. That's when the best part of the evening started."

"What happened?" asked Janice.

"Paul had never been in my new car, and when he saw it he was thrilled."

Larry had bought a convertible a few weeks ago. With his new attitude of thinking outside the box, he made a vow that as long as he was able to drive, he would have a convertible.

"So I asked Paul, 'Should I put the top down?'

"Of course he said, 'Sure!' So in a few minutes we were driving along Wilshire Boulevard with the top down, the stars bright, and the radio blasting jazz.

"Paul was sitting back and tapping his knee with his eyes closed. He opened his eyes, gave me a big smile, and said, 'Two cool dudes doing the town!'

"I have rarely felt so complimented," said Larry, "and I have really started to refire our relationship."

"So what did you learn from this experience?" asked Janice.

"I'm learning that even though I thought I was open to new experiences, I still have a ways to go. As you would guess, my idea would have been to go out to a restaurant where I'm comfortable—where I know what the rules are, what to order, and what to expect.

Going to a sushi restaurant with Paul—in an area I didn't know—made me feel uncomfortable."

"But you decided to go for it," said Janice with a smile.

"You bet I did! And it was one of the best things that's ever happened between Paul and me. Now I have to figure out how to take it to the next level."

Over the next three months, Larry and Janice refired their relationships—trying new things, connecting with their neighbors, looking for the pearls in people, and reaching out to old friends in new ways.

After a particularly fun night at a concert with some friends they hadn't seen in years, Janice said, "I've been having so much more fun since we've made a conscious effort to love and connect with people and try new experiences. If we keep this up, we'll have to call Wendy and Harold and tell them what's been happening with us around refiring emotionally."

PAUSE, REFLECT, TAKE ACTION

- When was the last time you ventured out of your comfort zone, and what did you do?
- What new things have you thought about doing but have not acted on?
- If you were going to start your own Last-Minute Gang, who would you invite?
- When will you begin?

- Choose one other person/couple to help you start a Last-Minute Gang and contact them.

5

Nothing Ordinary

A few weeks later, Larry and Janice met with the Tongs to give them a progress report.

"So how is your refiring journey going?" Harold asked, handing Larry and Janice glasses of iced tea.

"We think we've taken some real strides toward refiring emotionally," said Larry.

"Tell us about it," said Wendy.

"Ever since our meeting with you, Larry and I have made a concerted effort to make our important relationships—with each other, our friends, and our family—even better," said Janice. "We've become more spontaneous. We're reaching out, opening ourselves up to new opportunities, and looking for ways to break the patterns we've developed with so many people—including ourselves—of doing the same things in the same way, in the same places."

"We've even begun to develop a refiring code of conduct," said Larry. He handed them a piece of paper that read:

REFIRING CODE OF CONDUCT

Refiring Emotionally

- **Be playful ...** Laugh and kid
- **Be friendly ...** Smile and be happy
- **Be joyful ...** Embrace the moment
- **Be loving ...** Approach and welcome others
- **Be spontaneous ...** Get out of your comfort zone
- **Be enthusiastic ...** Give it your all

After reading the list, Wendy looked up and said, "That's marvelous!"

"We try to read it together every morning," said Janice. "Then we reread it at night before we go to bed, to see how well we have done to refire ourselves emotionally."

"I love that strategy—setting goals in the morning and then each night seeing how well you did that day," said Harold.

"Some days it doesn't work out because of schedule conflicts, but we do it more often than not," said Larry.

Wendy handed the paper back to Larry. "Let us hear about some of the specific things you decided to do to make your relationships better—how you're breaking old patterns and refiring your relationship with each other as well as with your family and good friends."

"We remembered when our kids were still at home," said Janice. "Every week we would ask one of them to choose a restaurant we would go to that weekend. We told them that no matter what kind of restaurant it was—or where it was or what was on the menu—we would go."

"And as I recall we had some pretty awful meals," said Larry.

"True," said Janice, "but we had some pretty good ones, too. I remember when we went to a Hungarian restaurant out in East County. We were the only ones there who spoke English. As I recall, none of us knew what we were eating, and we certainly couldn't pronounce the names of the dishes. But that was one of the best meals I've ever had. So last week I suggested to Larry that if the Hungarian place was still open, we should go there again."

"It was hard for Janice to believe, but I jumped at the opportunity and we went there the next night," said Larry. "Then we made a list of other restaurants we wanted to try and began brainstorming ideas about some things we could do that are new and different to refire our relationship."

"Good stuff," said Harold.

"To support our refiring efforts, we based all our decisions on the primary tenet of the Last-Minute Gang," said Janice.

Wendy looked puzzled. "The Last-Minute Gang?"

"Yes," said Janice. "It's a group of us who've decided that unless there's a compelling reason to say no to a new experience, we say yes—even at the last minute."

"I love that!" said Wendy.

"Then we took it even further," said Larry. "We decided that anytime we were asked to do something different, see something we hadn't seen before, or go someplace new, our mantra should be 'Why not? Why wait?'"

"That's brilliant!" Wendy said with enthusiasm.

Janice added, "And we asked ourselves: what if we went beyond *that* and put ourselves into situations that were totally unfamiliar to either of us—but might be fun?"

"Sounds great," said Harold.

"We also decided to adopt the Nothing Ordinary rule," said Larry.

"What's the Nothing Ordinary rule?" Harold asked.

"It's a commitment to uniqueness," Janice explained. "We realized that we have so much *stuff,* individually and together. We decided that when we go shopping for something, like clothing or things for the house, our rule will be not to choose anything *ordinary."*

"Who decides what's ordinary?" asked Wendy.

"Larry does, or I do, or we decide together. Either one of us can declare something 'not ordinary.'"

"So when we decide to get something new, it's special—that's the idea," said Larry.

"Then we had another great idea," said Janice. "We decided to think and act like tourists."

"And that means?" Harold prodded.

"We do what we do when we're going to a new city. We research where we're going, ask people for ideas about what's interesting to see and do, and then we see those places and do those things."

"We realized," said Larry, "that for the twenty years we've lived here, we've pretty much gone to the same parts of town, the same shops, and the same theaters. We've gone on the same walks and eaten in the same coffee shops and restaurants. In the meantime, lots of new things have happened. New neighborhoods and night spots have cropped up. There's live theater, music, and who knows what. In the past, unless we were invited by someone else, we didn't go to any of these new places."

"Can you give me an example?" asked Wendy.

"Sure," said Janice. "A good example is the Segway tour downtown."

"Segway?" asked Harold. "Where is Segway?"

"It's not a place," explained Larry. "It's new mode of transportation. I'm sure you've seen it on TV. You stand up on it. It's motorized, so when you lean forward, it moves forward and when you lean back, it stops."

Janice jumped in. "We saw an ad in the paper about touring downtown on the Segway. At first we laughed about it, and then we realized this was a perfect opportunity to get out of our comfort zone and do something new. We talked our friend Rob into going with us."

"What was amazing," said Larry, "is that we've lived in this town more than twenty years and we saw things on that tour we'd never seen before."

"That's hysterical," said Harold. "I can just see Larry gritting his teeth as he gets on the thing."

"There was definitely a learning curve," said Larry with a laugh.

"And I want to compliment you, Larry," said Janice, "because I really didn't think you'd give it a try. But you did. And look how much fun we had."

"It sounds to me," said Wendy," that you guys aren't focusing so much on *what* you do but on *how you're approaching* what you do. You're choosing not to do what's routine, easy, and most convenient, but rather forcing yourselves to stretch and inviting each other to test new, fun, or potentially interesting ideas and ways of doing things."

"Yes, you guys have challenged yourselves and made real progress in refiring emotionally," said Harold.

PAUSE, REFLECT, TAKE ACTION

- How can you apply the Nothing Ordinary rule to at least one aspect of your life?
- It's been said that the only way to avoid making a mistake is to never do anything new. If that is how you're living your life, what can you do to change?
- The next time you go to a restaurant, ask the server what is the best thing the restaurant serves—and order it.
- Take a car ride, no more than thirty minutes, to somewhere you've never been.
- Whenever you go out to buy something new, make sure it's special—Nothing Ordinary.

The Second Key

Refiring Intellectually

6

Mental Stimulation and Challenge

Driving home from the Tongs', Larry said, "I'm really feeling good about the progress I've made on this emotional thing."

"We've made," Janice corrected with a smile.

"Right, *we.* I'm also feeling good about us," he said.

"Me, too," said Janice.

"But," said Larry, "I'm also feeling kind of empty. Since stepping back from running the company, I feel adrift, like I don't really have a purpose or a place anymore."

"It's funny you mention that, because believe it or not, even though I've taken on this new job, I'm feeling much the same. One of the things about being the executive director is that I'm spending a lot of time doing paperwork. Frankly, the job is not as challenging or stimulating as I thought it would be."

"It sounds like we're both feeling unfulfilled," said Larry. "Are we missing something?"

"Maybe we can ask Dr. Jeffrey about that," said Janice.

"Good idea," said Larry.

***

"So how is your refiring journey going?" Dr. Jeffrey asked.

"As we were telling the Tongs, in a lot of ways, we've made real progress. We're challenging ourselves and each another," Larry said. "Even with our sex life."

With that last remark, Dr. Jeffrey's eyes lit up. He smiled and said, "As a researcher of aging, I'm always interested in the sex life of older adults. Tell me more about that."

Larry laughed and Janice blushed.

"At first, we were a little reluctant to talk about it," said Larry.

"But when we did," Janice jumped in, "we realized that when it came to making love, we did what was comfortable."

"That's right," said Larry. "We pretty much were doing the same thing, in the same place, often on the same night of the week. And you know what I told Janice? 'I think we can do better than this.'"

"After some candid conversations and with the help of our imaginations"—Janice paused to search for the right words—"the outcome has been positive. Need we say more?"

"Bravo!" said Dr. Jeffrey. "Most couples, as they mature together, don't talk about sex—much less do something about it."

Larry cleared his throat. "Enough about sex. The reason we came back to see you today is that I think we need a little more help in other areas."

"Maybe a lot more," said Janice.

"I'm all ears," said Dr. Jeffrey.

Janice continued, "So I told you last time I had this new job. What I'm finding is that this success thing isn't all it's cracked up to be."

"Nor is this cutting back on work thing," Larry interjected. "As I said to Janice, I'm feeling a little adrift."

"It sounds to me," said Dr. Jeffrey, "that while you two are growing emotionally, you may have to do more."

"Like what?" asked Janice.

"In addition to refiring emotionally, you also have to refire intellectually," said Dr. Jeffrey. "Growing intellectually is like oxygen to a deep-sea diver: without it, you die," said Dr. Jeffrey. "If you're not continuing to learn, you might as well lie down and let them throw the dirt on you, because you're already brain dead."

"Why don't you tell us what you really think about the importance of refiring intellectually?" said Larry with a laugh.

"You're right—I really do think intellectual growth is important. I'd like you to talk to Maria and Alberto Alvarez, two beautiful examples of older adults who are refiring intellectually. My assistant can give you their contact information. After you've seen them and thought about or perhaps been inspired to act on what they suggest, let's get together again, so I can hear the results."

"Sounds good," said Larry. "And thanks again. We could really use some help, ideas, direction, *something*—to get out of this funk we're in."

***

The Alvarezes lived in a sleek, high-rise condominium downtown with a view of the bay. As soon as Larry and Janice saw their smiles, they knew what wonderful, down-to-earth people Maria and Alberto were.

"Come right in," said Alberto. "We're so glad to meet you both."

"Yes," Maria added with a smile, "anyone who's a friend of Dr. Jeffrey can't be all bad. You must be exploring how to make the most of the coming years, or he wouldn't have sent you to us."

"You got it," said Larry as they settled into a comfortable seating area in the Alvarezes' living room.

"We're in a bit of a funk right now, "said Larry. "I've just cut back on work, while Janice has stepped into a leadership position at her nonprofit."

"Surprisingly, even though we've moved in different directions, we're both experiencing a letdown," said Janice.

Larry said, "Dr. Jeffrey suggested that it was a head issue. He told us that if we didn't begin to refire intellectually, our ability to think and solve problems might decline and we could end up walking around half dead, like zombies."

Janice shook her head with a laugh. "That's a little exaggeration of what he said, but he did emphasize the importance of staying active intellectually. Since he sent us to you as great examples, could you tell us what you do to keep your minds sharp?"

Maria and Alberto looked at each other and smiled.

"We definitely support each other that way," said Alberto. "We just celebrated our fiftieth wedding anniversary."

"Congratulations!" said Janice. "You've got us beat by a few years."

Maria said, "Alberto and I met in college and we've been a team ever since—encouraging each other's intellectual growth."

"Let me tell you a little about us," said Alberto. "Maria and I started a leadership development and consulting company over thirty years ago. Maria really knows how to make things happen, so she became president. I have a background in finance but my real passion is setting the vision and cheering people on, so I became the chief spiritual officer. After about ten years in business, Maria's brother joined us as chief operating officer. Our son and daughter joined us shortly after that and got involved in product development and sales. We formed a family council and the five of us began to run the company together."

"So you have a real family business," said Larry.

"Absolutely," said Alberto. "A few years ago we decided it was time to transfer the key leadership responsibilities to Maria's brother and our two kids.

"We didn't want to ride off into the sunset," continued Alberto, "so we had to find a way to refire, as you put it—particularly intellectually."

"Sometimes I feel like I am riding off into the sunset, because I feel out of it," said Larry. "What did you do that I'm not doing?"

"It sounds like you're taking a big step back from work, is that right?" asked Alberto.

"Yes," said Larry.

"I decided not to do that," said Alberto. "I transitioned from my executive duties to explore other ways I could contribute within the organization, like mentoring young leaders. This gave me time to use some of the skills I had running my company to make a difference in the community."

"In what way?" asked Janice.

"I was tired of everyone complaining about how badly our city was run, but I knew I didn't want to run for office. So I took a course on public administration at the university to better understand what government could do. I saw that there was a role for me on the financial side. So I volunteered to work in the office of Councilman Chin, who chairs the City Council's budget committee."

"Wow, that's great," said Larry. "Fred Baker at the Small Business Administration has been hounding me for years to do some volunteer mentoring for young entrepreneurs. I've always wanted to do it—I guess now is the time."

"That's a great plan," said Alberto. "I'm sure the SBA can use your help."

"I did things a little differently," said Maria. "I decided to refire intellectually by staying on at the company. A few years ago I became aware that to be in business today, you have to manage the present and create the future at the same time."

"What do you mean?" asked Janice.

"Most organizations task people with present-time responsibilities to plan the future. When you do that, the people doing the planning kill the future, because they either have a vested interest in the present or are overwhelmed by it.

"That intrigued me," Maria continued, "and it also seemed very important. Knowing this was becoming truer every day, I mobilized a couple of other people to join me in creating an Office of the Future, where we study new trends in the economy, society, technology—you name it. At our industry's national convention, my colleagues and I make it a practice to walk the exhibit hall and examine the small booths, where most of the new ideas are generated. I constantly have my eyes on the horizon, so I'm continually refiring intellectually."

"So you're not just sitting around vegetating," said Janice.

"That's for sure!" said Alberto. "Maria and her colleagues have been invaluable in keeping the company on top of the latest innovations with the Internet, teleconferencing, and emerging technologies for staying in touch with clients."

"Not only has it been important for the company, but it's also been important for me. I'm excited about learning again," said Maria.

"I can see how you two have created a life that keeps you mentally active," said Janice, "but what about people who don't have our options and aren't in the position to create their own intellectually stimulating positions?"

"No matter what your occupation or position in life," said Alberto, "you can create a plan—a curriculum, as it were—to refire intellectually. Whether it's taking classes, joining a book club, taking courses at a nearby university, or immersing yourself in another culture, you can keep your brain cells stimulated."

"You've inspired me," said Larry. "I'm going to stop complaining and call up the SBA tomorrow."

"And Maria," said Janice, "hearing you talk about what you did in your company makes me realize that I need to do the same thing in my nonprofit. Maybe I can turn over the paperwork to someone else and do the future-oriented work in our organization that you're doing in your company. Can I call you for pointers when I get into it?"

"Absolutely!" said Maria.

"Sounds like you each have a plan," said Alberto. "How are you going to support each other?"

"That's a good question," said Janice. "Remember, Larry, I may be spending more time at the office getting this thing off the ground."

"Go for it!" said Larry. "And by the way, I may be spending more time in meetings."

"I'll pack you a lunch," Janice said with a smile.

"Dr. Jeffrey was right to hold you up as examples," said Larry. "You two are inspiring us to refire intellectually on all cylinders! Thanks so much for sharing your stories."

"Our pleasure," Maria said as she showed them to the door. "Keep us posted on your progress."

"We will," Janice promised.

With that, Larry and Janice bid adieu to their new friends.

***

It was late afternoon as Larry and Janice drove away from the Alvarezes.

"Why don't we have an early dinner at that new restaurant we heard about in town?" said Larry.

"Good idea," said Janice. "It will give us plenty of time to review what we learned from Alberto and Maria and continue developing our own plans for refiring intellectually."

For the next several minutes they talked about how much they admired the Alvarezes and discussed their plans for staying mentally stimulated and challenged. Larry pointed out that Alberto's work with the city not only kept him mentally stimulated, but also fulfilled the generosity aspect of moving from success to significance that Dr. Jeffrey had talked about. Eventually the conversation died down and the car fell silent as they became lost in their own thoughts.

As they neared downtown, Larry broke the silence. "So what are you going to order for dinner?" he asked.

Janice didn't look up as she answered distractedly, "Oh, I don't know. I'll see what's on the menu. Maybe they'll have some specials."

"What are you doing?" asked Larry, although he already knew what she was doing.

"Just texting the kids. I haven't heard from them in a while and I just wanted to say hello and let them know what's going on."

"Why don't you just call them? We've got this Bluetooth® thing in the car so you can talk to them and I can listen, and we can have a real conversation."

"Well, you know Eileen is pretty busy these days. I think at times she resents our calling. When I text, she can read it when she's ready and then get back to me at her convenience."

"I think that texting stuff is a bunch of baloney," said Larry. "Besides, it's too much trouble. I'm not going to spend my time typing *hello* on those tiny keys when I can just pick up the phone and say, 'Hello!' Some people like smartphones but I prefer a dumb phone. I can call people and they can call me. I don't even like voicemail. It just bugs me."

Janice put down her phone and gave Larry a long, hard look. "I guess when it comes to refiring intellectually, I'm going to be the one who embraces the future, like Maria. I want to learn about all the new technology and new ways to communicate. It would be fun if learning about new technology was a mutual goal of ours, but I doubt it will be."

"That's for sure," said Larry.

Janice sighed. "When it comes to technology, Larry, you sound like an old codger. This is too new; that's too complicated; you can't learn this; you don't like that. What's going on here? When the grandkids were down a couple weeks ago, you banned them from using any gadgets—no texting, no emails, no cell phones, no using their tablets—and they really resented you for that."

"The way I see it," said Larry, "is when people are together they should be talking to one another, not playing games or reading books or texting or sending emails or whatever. That's just impolite, and it really irritates me when I see it going on."

"Why do you think that irritates you so much, Larry? You aren't someone who generally gets angry, but this seems to really get to you. Is it that you don't know how to do those things and are afraid you can't learn?"

Larry remembered the first conversation they'd had with Dr. Jeffrey, who'd pointed out that many older people are reluctant to try new things, be with different people, or put themselves in unfamiliar situations. Their unconscious first response to doing something new and different was to say no. At the time Larry hadn't thought that applied to him, but his sushi dinner with his grandson Paul had taught him a valuable lesson.

After a long pause Larry said, "You know, I hate to admit it, but you may be right. This new electronic gadget world is taking over. People don't talk—they tweet; they Instagram; they email; they text. I can't keep up! Everybody's on Facebook. Rob asked me if I was on LinkedIn, and Sandy asked me for my Twitter account. There's all this stuff, and you can bet there's more coming. I'm not certain it's a good thing, and I'm not sure I want to get involved." With that Larry pulled into a parking space near the new restaurant.

"Larry, you're being a stick in the mud again. If I'm going to be looking to the future, you can't be looking at the past—particularly if you're going to mentor entrepreneurs at the SBA."

Once they were inside and at their table, Janice reached over and patted Larry's hand.

"I'm proud of you for suggesting we come to this restaurant," she said. "Remember last week you told me about asking one of your colleagues to join you for lunch at that great sushi place? When she told you she only liked American food and didn't go to ethnic restaurants, you pointed out how rigid she was and how surprised you were by her lack of openness to new experiences. But in some ways, I'm wondering if you aren't still a little bit like that with new technology."

Larry remained silent.

Janice continued, "We certainly have made some real strides with our Last-Minute Gang policy and our Nothing Ordinary philosophy. Those new approaches have already made a difference in our relationships and our emotional lives. We need to bring that same mindset to refiring our intellectual lives."

Larry finally broke his silence. "I think you have a point there. I need to continue to be more open about learning new things. Alberto and Maria inspired me that way."

Janice squeezed his hand and said, "I'm so happy to hear you say that. I was a little worried about how our conversation was going in the car. I don't want us to slip and look at aging as a downhill slide. Since we've been focused on refiring, I've noticed certain things are pretty typical for people as they get older—like losing keys or forgetting what you were looking for when you go into a room. That's just part of aging. But that doesn't mean we can't continue to learn and grow intellectually."

"I'm with you," said Larry. "Let's figure out what each of us can do on our own to learn new things and refire our minds."

Janice smiled. "As I said earlier, I'm the future gal, so I'll learn as much as I can about all the new technological changes. And if you're good, I'll even mentor you into the twenty-first century."

Their server approached the table. She introduced herself with a smile and asked, "What can I get for you folks?"

"What are your specials?" asked Janice. "I'm going to try something really different."

"Me, too," said Larry.

As they were waiting for their "different" meal, Janice said, "I like your idea to mentor young entrepreneurs at the Small Business Administration. What else do you think you'll do to refire intellectually?"

"I've been thinking about writing," said Larry.

"Writing! Like what?" Janice asked, her eyes brightening.

"A family history—yours and ours. I've even got a title for it: *Enduring Love.*"

"That's sweet," said Janice. "How will you begin?"

"I'll bet the university has a course in creative writing," said Larry. "Rather than just hearing a lecture or two, I'd like to take a real class with real students."

"What a great idea!" said Janice.

"A colleague of mine was telling me recently that there's a way where any person can take any class being offered to regular students, so long as they get the permission of the instructor."

"I didn't know that," said Janice. "I wonder if there are any classes in pottery. Learning to make vases and bowls has been a desire of mine for quite a while."

"I'll bet the university has classes in creative arts in their continuing education offerings," said Larry.

"You're probably right. For a long time now we've been driving past the university. It's about time we explored it and maybe even became part of it," said Janice.

"That's an exciting idea," said Larry. "We don't want to be one of those couples that are always talking about what they *used* to do, what they *used* to learn, what they *used* to know. Let's get back into the world of thinking and doing."

"You're on," said Janice.

And that's exactly what they did.

Janice shared with their kids what they were up to and asked them to mentor her on all the new technology. Their son-in-law David found a grad student who was a real tech geek to help Janice master her new devices.

Larry found a creative writing course and signed up. He also found a freelance writer who could give him feedback and editorial help. He was really proud of himself—and also proud of Janice, whose artistic gifts were obvious, even in her first attempts at pottery.

A few months later, Janice proudly displayed her latest handiwork.

"How do you like my new vase?" she asked.

"That's really great!" said Larry. "This refiring intellectually isn't too bad."

***

Larry and Janice decided to stop by Dr. Jeffrey's office to share their excitement.

He gave them his usual warm welcome and said, "How is my refiring team? Have you added on to your Refiring Code of Conduct?"

"We sure have," said Janice as she proudly turned on her new tablet and showed a document to Dr. Jeffrey.

REFIRING INTELLECTUALLY

- **Be open to learn ...** Look for learning in every situation
- **Be a reader ...** Constantly search for new information
- **Be teachable ...** Let others mentor you
- **Be courageous ...** Venture into new areas
- **Be persistent ...** Stay with it even when it's difficult

Dr. Jeffrey nodded his approval. "That's great. And I love that you're using a tablet now."

"It's fun," said Janice. "My kids are keeping me up-to-date and are forcing me to master this thing."

"I'm even overcoming my technophobia," said Larry. "Now that Janice has learned all about the new technology, she's teaching me how to use these new electronic gadgets. I've decided I'm going to become as smart as my phone. She's shown me how to text and use some of the apps. I've joined Facebook—can you believe it?—and I'm even learning to Skype, so I can talk with our grandkids on the computer, even if they're across the country. At this rate I might even learn to Twitter!"

"You mean tweet," said Janice.

"Yeah, yeah. Twitter, tweet—however you say it."

Larry, Janice, and Dr. Jeffrey had a big laugh.

"Tell me more about your intellectual journey," said Dr. Jeffrey.

Excitedly, Larry shared his plans for writing a family history and mentoring entrepreneurs. Then Janice chimed in to share about refiring her position at the nonprofit and becoming a potter.

"You guys are doing great. Keep it up," said Dr. Jeffrey.

PAUSE, REFLECT, TAKE ACTION

- What can you do to make your present life more interesting and challenging?
- What new technology might you embrace, and who can help you learn it?
- Make a list of the things that used to excite you—for example, acting, photography, model building, poetry, or writing.
- How can you bring one of these passions back into your life?
- Either in person or online, take one class in an area you know little or nothing about.

The Third Key

Refiring Physically

7

A Moment of Truth

Janice was fixing dinner when Larry walked through the door. "Hey," was all he could manage.

"What's the matter with you?" she asked. "You look like you've seen a ghost. Is everything okay?"

"Not really," Larry replied. "I just got a call from my doctor's office. I have diabetes."

"You have *what?*" she asked.

"Diabetes. This is serious, Janice. The doctor said that left untreated, a diabetes patient can go blind or lose a limb—or a kidney, even."

Now Janice was the one looking shell-shocked. "Just like that, out of the blue, you have diabetes?"

Larry shook his head. "I knew I'd been more tired than usual, and I'd been hitting the men's room more often, but I had no idea it was this serious."

"What's the doctor's prognosis? Does he think you'll be okay?"

"The doctor said it's up to me. He can give me meds, but that's only a temporary solution. If I want to keep this from getting worse, I have to make changes—diet, exercise, all the things I know I should be doing."

***

"So," said Dr. Jeffrey. "I didn't expect to see you guys so soon again."

"We didn't expect to be back this soon, either," said Larry, "but when I found out I had diabetes—"

"Type 1 or type 2?" asked Jeffrey.

"Type 2."

"Oh, the lifestyle-change diabetes."

"You got it," said Larry. "I've got to clean up my act."

"To be fair," said Janice, "it's not only Larry who needs to make changes."

"Why do you say that?" asked Larry.

"Remember when I had lunch with my friend Charlotte the other day and I came home looking so upset?"

"Yes," said Larry. "For a minute I thought it was something I did."

"It wasn't about you. Getting to the restaurant had been a real hassle. Downtown was so crowded I couldn't find a parking place. When I finally did find one, it must have been ten blocks from the restaurant. By the time I got there, I was sweaty, tired, and irritable."

"I remember you telling me what an ordeal that was for you," said Larry.

"I knew what Larry was thinking," Janice said to Dr. Jeffrey. "He was thinking that part of the reason I got so tired was that I haven't been exercising."

"But I didn't say a thing," said Larry.

"You didn't have to," said Janice. "Like I said, I knew what you were thinking."

"So you're a mind reader?" kidded Dr. Jeffrey. "You really know what Larry's thinking?"

"No, I guess I knew what *I* was thinking. I haven't been taking very good care of myself, either," Janice admitted.

Larry turned to Janice and said in a gentle tone, "You know, during the reunion weekend, I think we both did a pretty good job of eating well and staying active. But after that, it seems to me you got a bit overwhelmed with your new position and let everything about your health slip."

"Yep," said Janice. "As I said, I've known for a while that I need to make some changes—and so do you. Remember how you complained that the cleaners shrank your best pants?"

"Yes," said Larry.

"The cleaner didn't shrink your pants and make them tight. The pants didn't shrink—you grew!"

Dr. Jeffrey began to laugh and then stopped himself. "Sounds like you both need to refire physically," he said.

"You're probably right," said Janice. "But it seems like it will be a lot of work—like we'll have to turn our lives upside down," said Janice.

"Maybe," said Dr. Jeffrey. "But it may be easier than you think, once you both make the commitment."

"What do you have in mind?" asked Larry.

"You've both gained weight and don't exercise. Is that right?" asked Dr. Jeffrey.

"I try to exercise," said Larry. "But I have to admit, I think about it more than I do it."

"My exercise program has been nonexistent," confessed Janice.

"The combination of eating too much and not exercising enough has led to your fatigue, Janice, and the same habits have contributed to your developing diabetes, Larry."

"Given those facts, the question is: what should we be doing?" wondered Janice. "I don't want to go on one of those crazy diet programs where you eat nothing but X in the morning and don't have any Y in the evening and don't get to eat anything you like."

"Me, either," Larry chimed in. "I don't want to go on any kind of program that's nothing but twigs, nuts, and green vegetables."

The three of them laughed.

"I guess we want the results but aren't willing to change what we do," said Larry.

"You may be right," said Dr. Jeffrey. "But I do have some ideas."

"Like what?" asked Janice.

"I think the place to start is exercise, as opposed to trying to deal with food."

"Why do you say that?" said Larry.

"Because once you've exercised, nobody can take it away from you," said Dr. Jeffrey. "On the other hand, when you try to lose weight by cutting calories, you can be perfect twenty-three and a half hours and then blow it in the last half hour. So I suggest you start with exercise. It's easier to just jump in and do."

"Okay, I'm for that," said Larry.

"I want you two to begin taking the *minimally effective dose."*

"What in the world does that mean?" asked Janice.

"Taking the minimally effective dose means figuring out exactly what you need to do to get the effect you want," Dr. Jeffrey explained.

"That sounds like doing nothing," said Larry.

"But it's not," said Dr. Jeffrey. "The minimally effective dose means doing just enough, but not anything more."

Janice said, "To be honest, I've always hated the idea of having to go to a gym, working out with other people, spending a half hour getting there, changing clothes, and then coming home to put myself together."

"That's not what you need to do," said Dr. Jeffrey. "For people your age, who are dealing with the age-typical medical problems, the minimally effective dose of exercise is walking five to six days a week, thirty to forty-five minutes a day."

"You've got to be kidding," said Janice. "That's all?"

"I'm not kidding, that's all," said Dr. Jeffrey. "That doesn't mean that either of you can't choose to do more exercise, if you want to."

"I'd like to make a suggestion," said Larry.

"What?" said Janice with suspicion.

"Since both of us get up early in the morning anyway and neither of us has to start the day at the crack of dawn, let's experiment with taking a walk every morning. If it's rainy or cold, we can go to the Y and use the treadmills there. We can start off with thirty minutes and then add five minutes a week until we decide it's enough. And that will be our minimally effective exercise dose," said Larry.

"But what if it's not enough?" said Janice.

"You can check this out with your physician, of course, but I have a lot of older patients, so I know a lot about this," said Dr. Jeffrey. "According to the research I've been reading, it will likely be enough. If you get some good shoes, wear the right clothes, and walk regularly, my guess is you're both going to begin to feel better. You won't be so tired, Janice. And this will help control your diabetes, Larry.

"As a matter of fact," Dr. Jeffrey continued, "I read that less than 20 percent of people over sixty-five do any exercise on a regular basis. If you commit to walking, you'll be fitter than 80 percent of your age group. Wouldn't that be great?"

"Okay," said Janice. "We'll start off with exercise. What's next?"

"My doctor says I need to lose about twenty pounds," said Larry.

"I'd like to lose about fifteen," added Janice.

"Those are achievable goals," said Dr. Jeffrey. "I suggest that you first stop eating and drinking *mindlessly* and begin eating and drinking *mindfully."*

"Mindlessly, mindfully—what are you talking about?" asked Larry.

"Tell me about what you eat at night," said Dr. Jeffrey.

"Larry won't like me telling you this, but before we sit down to eat, Larry has a drink and then usually one or two glasses of wine with dinner. Almost every night, he has a second portion of whatever we're eating. And the last thing he says is, 'What's for dessert?'"

Dr. Jeffrey turned to Larry. "Three drinks a night, plus dessert, in addition to what you eat for the meal, is obviously too much. I'm guessing this way of eating and drinking has become a habit. You're probably not even aware you're drinking that much."

"You're right," said Larry. "But I don't want to stop drinking entirely. Besides, I read that drinking one or two glasses of red wine a night helps to prevent heart attacks."

"You don't have a heart problem, Sweetie, you have diabetes," said Janice.

"I suggest you switch to water or sugar-free iced tea with your meals and a glass or two of wine at social occasions," said Dr. Jeffrey. "That's how you can begin to be mindful about drinking."

"I have some ideas about how we can be more mindful about what I cook," said Janice. "You tell me if I'm on the right track, Dr. Jeffrey."

"No grass or twigs," said Larry ominously.

"No, no grass and twigs, but I am going to make some changes, some of which you will be aware of, and some that you won't."

Larry frowned. "Changes? Like what?"

"To begin with, I can cook differently. I can figure out a way to not make cream sauces and sugary desserts. Tell you what—I'll let you be the exercise guru. How about if you let me be the food guru? I'll make sure we become more aware of when, how, and why we eat. Let's also try cutting back 20 percent of how much we eat."

"How much we eat?"

"Janice has a good point," said Dr. Jeffrey. "It's not just *what* you eat; it's also how *much* you eat."

"I think it's really easy to mindlessly eat more than we really need to," said Janice. "How often do we keep eating until we feel full or stuffed, as opposed to eating until we feel good and satisfied?"

"That's another good point," said Dr. Jeffrey. "There's a big difference between being stuffed and being satisfied. If you eat until you're full, you've eaten too much, but if you eat until you're satisfied and then stop, you're paying attention to what your body is telling you."

"Okay, I'll give it a try," said Larry.

"And I promise you one thing," said Janice, "everything I cook will taste really good. There will be no diet foods—no twigs and nuts. So we'll be eating less, enjoying it more, and losing weight."

Janice turned to Dr. Jeffrey. "One other thing—I have a bad habit of eating late at night, especially when I'm feeling stressed or tired or worried. I'm going to have to deal with that problem on my own."

"That's not a problem of mine," said Larry.

"I know," said Janice. "That's why I'm saying it's my issue, not yours. I'll have to figure out what I can do instead of eating when I'm feeling upset."

"Okay, I think we have some good plans. Maybe we're done here," said Larry.

"What do you mean done?" asked Dr. Jeffrey.

"If we get on a good exercise program and I cook healthier meals, Larry and I will both lose weight. Seems to me that's what Larry means—that we're on our way to refiring physically."

"You're off to a good start," said Dr. Jeffrey. "But I think you have a couple of other things that you need to deal with if you're serious about getting healthy."

"Oh, my, that sounds serious," said Janice.

"It is," said Dr. Jeffrey. "But I don't want to minimize the importance of what you've committed to do. The aerobic exercise you've been talking about is necessary for cardiovascular health. And as you already implied, it is the best way to burn off calories and, in the process, body fat. In terms of nutrition and weight control, no matter how much exercise you do, unless you focus on what you eat, you'll never be at the weight you desire or attain optimal health. So your plans for both those areas are good.

"But besides aerobic exercise, nutrition, and weight control," continued Dr. Jeffrey, "there are four more components of a complete health and fitness program."

"What are they?" asked Larry.

"Flexibility, balance training, rest/sleep, and strength training."

"Strength training?" said Larry. "You want me to bulk up and develop big muscles?"

"Rather than me answering questions like that, why don't you go see a coach at the downtown YMCA? I can refer you to the guy who heads up their fitness training program. I'll call him and tell him to expect a visit from you. Before you go to see him, I recommend that each of you make an appointment with your doctor to let him know what you're planning to do."

"We'll do it," said Janice. "Right, Larry?"

"Right," said Larry.

"Your doctor is also better qualified than a coach to talk to you about the importance of sleep and rest."

"I like the idea of Janice going to see our doctor," said Larry. "But she doesn't always do what he says."

"What do you mean?" said Janice.

"You know what I mean," Larry replied. "I know that you hate to think about this, but what are you doing about your high blood pressure?"

Janice frowned. "What do you mean, what am I doing? I saw Dr. Fredrick and he prescribed some medication, and that's that."

"That's that?" asked Larry.

"Yes, that's that," said Janice.

"I know he prescribed medication, but that's not the issue. The issue is whether or not you take the medication," Larry said.

"You know I hate taking medication, Larry. Besides, I feel just fine."

"I know you feel just fine, but as Dr. Fredrick said, with high blood pressure there don't have to be symptoms."

"I think Larry's right," said Dr. Jeffrey. "You should do what the doctor prescribes."

"I know you're right," said Janice. "I should be taking my blood pressure every day and recording it, so when I see the doctor he knows what's been going on. I also should be taking my medications. I know,

I know, I know. I just wish Larry would stop nagging me about it."

"Nagging?" said Larry. "I haven't nagged once. It seems to me that not talking about your high blood pressure and not taking your medication means you're avoiding something that's really important. And now Dr. Jeffrey is suggesting we go to Dr. Frederick before we start to refire physically."

"I guess losing weight and exercising will lower my blood pressure," said Janice.

"Probably," said Dr. Jeffrey. "That's something I would ask your doctor. Until you see him, how about you make a commitment to take your medicine every day and check your blood pressure a few times a week?"

Janice fiddled with her wedding ring as she considered the question. Finally, she sighed and said, "Okay."

"So," said Dr. Jeffrey. "Once you get the okay from Dr. Frederick to start refiring physically, go see the coach at the Y."

"You've got a deal," said Larry.

***

After their meeting with Dr. Jeffrey, Larry and Janice realized that refiring physically could be tougher than refiring emotionally or intellectually.

Doing as Dr. Jeffrey suggested, they went to see Dr. Frederick. He gave Janice a mild reprimand for not taking her medicine and gave her a new prescription, but was happy to report that everything else with her health was fine. Larry got good news that his blood sugar levels were already lower. Dr. Frederick advised him to keep working on the changes he'd made and prescribed some oral medication. He not only okayed but also encouraged their new exercise program.

They kept their commitment to walk outside or on the treadmill five or six days a week for thirty to forty-five minutes—at least most of the time. There were a few weeks when their schedules got in the way of exercising. What got them back on track was that when they did their walking, they saw a positive difference in their muscle tone and energy levels. Also, they began to notice they felt bloated and less energetic when they didn't eat sensibly.

They also went to the coach at the YMCA and learned how to do some beginning strength, balance, and flexibility training.

PAUSE, REFLECT, TAKE ACTION

- Identify at least one way you can eat more healthfully.
- What's a first step you can take to becoming more physically active?
- What is the obstacle to doing that?
- How can you remove this obstacle?

• Set a modest goal, such as losing five pounds or walking a mile a day. Set a date to achieve this goal and start today!

8

Dealing with Setbacks

Larry and Janice had just loaded the last of the dinner plates into the dishwasher when the doorbell rang.

"That's Phil and Kelly," said Larry, "right on time for dessert and decaf."

Their good friends had been missing in action from the last few meetings of the Last-Minute Gang. When Janice called to follow up, Kelly explained they would be out of commission for a while because Phil was having some medical problems. Kelly hadn't been specific, and Janice hadn't pried.

"Welcome!" Janice said as she opened the door. Her smile turned to a look of surprise when she saw Phil. The man who had been one of the most vigorous people they knew was leaning on a walker. Kelly stood beside him, holding his arm protectively.

"Oh, my goodness, Phil. Are you okay? Is there anything we need to do for you?"

"No," said Phil with a laugh. "Just watch me gimp over to a chair, and as soon as I'm settled, everything will be fine."

Janice saw them into the living room, where a beverage and fruit tray had been set up. "How about some decaf and a fruit plate?" asked Janice.

"That sounds great," said Kelly.

"Pour one for me, too," said Phil.

Larry walked in from the kitchen and stopped in his tracks when he caught sight of Phil negotiating the transition from walker to sofa.

"Good grief, Phil, what happened to my golfing buddy?"

"Well," responded Phil. "I was walking around in my study when I suddenly got this incredible pain in my back and shooting pains down my leg. It just came out of nowhere."

"That's doesn't sound good," said Janice as she handed Phil his cup of decaf. "So what did you do?"

"In my usual way," said Phil, "I tried to ignore it—but the pain didn't go away. So I Googled 'back pain' to figure out what was going on. I tried to take care of myself by stretching and doing some floor exercises, which helped a little, but not much. When the pain got worse, I finally called our family doctor and told him what was going on."

"And?" prompted Larry.

"My doctor said it sounded as though I had some kind of a disc problem. He said that 90 percent of the time these kinds of problems resolved on their own. He told me not to worry about it. He suggested I take some ibuprofen, rest for a few days, and then get back to him and let him know how I was doing."

"So?" said Janice.

"Of course, I only paid half attention to what he said. Again I went online and began doing research on discs, pain in the legs, and so on. I saw that it might be something serious, but as my doctor said, 90 percent of the time it goes away. I cut back on golf and began resting more, but the pain was not going away."

"So then what did you do?" asked Larry.

Kelly intervened. "I could tell that Phil wasn't getting any better, so I urged him to call his doctor again. At that point his pain was so bad he was having difficulty sleeping and even having trouble getting dressed."

Phil took a sip of coffee. "To make a long story short, I went in, got an MRI, and was told I had a herniated disc and a bunch of other bad spine stuff that comes with aging. The doc said if I didn't have surgery, things could get worse and I might permanently lose some function in my right leg. I rested for a week and got a second opinion at the university's medical school, but there was no way around it—I had to have surgery. I went under the knife a month ago, and here I am on the road to recovery. Some road!"

Larry and Janice exchanged a look. Larry took a deep breath and said, "Man, Phil, that sounds rough."

Phil let out a cheerless laugh. "I'll say. It's been the most interesting, challenging, humbling, educational, painful, complicated experience of my life."

"In what way?" asked Janice.

"I've always been a healthy guy and have never had any serious medical problems. I'd never even been in the hospital as an adult and hadn't had an operation since my tonsillectomy when I was four years old. So going through this health crisis was not only new but also very, very scary. It might be less overwhelming for people who have been dealing with different illnesses over the years, but as someone who's always been healthy, I took it hard. It literally knocked me off my feet."

Larry nodded. "I can relate to that," he said. "That's how I felt when I got my diabetes diagnosis. What in particular was scary for you?"

"The surgery was more complicated than expected, which was frightening. My hospital stay was longer than anticipated, and all of the rosy assurances—that I'd be pain free in a few days, walking at the end of a week, back to myself in another week, and going to my office by the end of the month—proved to be overly optimistic. It scared me that I might not ever really get better."

"Phil has been having a really hard time," said Kelly. "He endured having to be in bed for over two weeks, which was a struggle, and he needed help getting dressed and even taking a shower. Fortunately, most of that is behind us. He hates using a walker. I feel powerless watching him try to figure out how to deal with all of this."

Janice offered Phil a plate of grapes and sliced melon. "I know at least two other people who've had back problems, but they don't talk about it very much."

"I can understand why," said Phil. "As we've shared my experience with others, we're finding out that back issues are fairly common. In fact, back pain is the leading cause of disability in Americans over forty-five, and as many as one in three people are going to have a back problem at some point after they're sixty-five."

"You said this has been a learning experience," said Larry. "In what way?"

"I'm learning that I'm not as infallible as I thought. I'm learning what it's really like to be in pain. I'm learning how to ask for help. I learned how to take a shower sitting down and have Kelly put my socks on, because I was prohibited from bending over for the first couple of weeks."

The room became silent.

Suddenly, Phil laughed out loud. "I'm appreciating on a whole new level what this refiring stuff is all about!"

And at that moment, the old Phil returned.

"I may not be able to take any more mountain climbing trips with my buddies," he continued, "but I'm sure going to be able to reach a place where I can take a walk on the beach with Kelly. At this point in my refiring journey, I'm not going to be able to work very much—particularly if it means sitting in a chair for hours at a time—because that's not what this body is capable of doing right now. On the bright side, this condition forces me to think about what other things I can do to get myself going."

"I wish I'd known what you were going through, Phil, so I could have helped out," said Janice.

"I didn't want to burden anyone," said Phil.

"So you've been suffering in silence," teased Larry.

"More or less," Phil admitted. "To be honest, I had to fight the temptation to give up."

"What do you mean?" asked Janice with a look of alarm.

"I got depressed and really down on myself. I kept trying to figure out why this had happened. I felt picked on by fate or God or who knows what, and was beginning to think of myself as a permanent invalid."

"But you know what?" said Kelly. "The kids would have none of it."

"The kids?" Larry and Janice said together.

"Yes, the kids. They called up their dad and told him they expected him to recover, that they would not accept his giving up. They said that while part of his recovery might depend on the outcome of his surgery, a lot of it would depend on how hard he was willing to work to gain his strength back, do physical therapy, and whatever else he had to do. They were supportive but straightforward. It was tough love all over again, but this time Phil was on the receiving end instead of dishing it out."

"It's true," added Phil. "The kids and I switched roles. Rather than me being there for them when they were in trouble, they were there for me."

Larry smiled. "I remember the first time that happened to me. A few years ago when I was still skiing, my youngest daughter had to slow down to wait for me and make sure I was okay, as opposed to my slowing down and waiting for her to make sure she was okay. It was a weird feeling."

Janice warmed up Phil's coffee. "So now that you're getting to the other side of all this, what have you learned?" she asked.

"I'm still learning," Phil replied. "I'm learning that bad things can happen to anyone—there aren't any guarantees or free passes in life. I'd said those words before, but now I really understand them. I've learned that it's easy to feel optimistic and ready to refire when you're feeling good, but not so easy when you're feeling bad. I've learned to appreciate the simpler things, like being able to come over here and visit with the two of you, or take a short walk in front of my house, or go to the movies, which I'll be able to do next week once I've gotten the okay to sit for a few hours at a time."

"I've learned a lot from this too," said Kelly.

"Such as?" Janice prodded.

"I've learned that no matter what your circumstances are, you still have a choice about how to deal with those circumstances. I learned that from seeing what a difference it made once Phil listened to his kids and turned his attitude around."

"It wasn't just the kids that turned me around," said Phil. "A lot of it was that I just got mad."

"Mad? What do you mean?" asked Larry.

"I got mad at myself for being a whiner. I got fed up with myself for being so passive and acting like a wimp, waiting for other people to come to my rescue. I just got mad."

"And when Phil gets mad," said Kelly with a smile, "you know what happens?"

"What?" asked Janice.

"His anger activates him. It gets him going. It's the opposite of when he's depressed, when he just sits around and mopes. When Phil gets angry, he gets creative. He reaches out and does the sorts of things that have made him successful in other parts of his life. It's one of the things I love about him."

"So I got mad and saw that my recovery was up to me," said Phil. "I couldn't wait for other people. The surgeon had done his thing, and now if I was going to do the things I wanted to do, I would have to stop sitting around moping and begin acting. I called up two friends who'd gone through the same type of operation, and both of them were now doing pretty well. My friend Don, who was six months postsurgery, said his healing had taken a long time, much longer than the surgeons had led him to believe. He was finally getting back into the swing of things and walking without any type of aid. My other friend, Walt, actually came over and visited. Like Don, his recovery had taken much longer than expected, but he was now living a full and active life, pretty much back to what he was doing, maybe at the 80 to 90 percent level."

"That was a great idea, getting encouragement from people who'd walked in your moccasins," said Janice. "Did they give you any pointers?"

"They both said that choosing a good physical therapist was really important, so we found someone who was personable and knowledgeable. I'm happy to report that I'm through my first week of physical therapy and I think it's going to work."

"Actually," said Kelly, "Phil has been off the walker for two weeks. We only brought it tonight because we didn't know how far away we'd have to park. But he's using the cane now and walking on his own."

Phil shook his head. "I'm amazed how tired I get after an hour of physical therapy, especially when I think about how much exercise I used to do."

"On the bright side," said Kelly, "we have been out to dinner."

"And in addition to a movie next week, believe it or not, we're going to a dinner dance next Saturday night. I'll have to come with a cane, though."

Kelly smiled. "And we probably won't be doing much dancing. But the point is we'll be there with our friends and back to living a real life."

"Way to go!" said Larry.

Kelly reached over and put her hand on Phil's arm. "This whole ordeal has taught us that refiring is not just for the hale and hearty; it's something you can do even if you're not 100 percent well. So much of our health and recovery from illness depends on our attitude. Phil and I have decided to accept what comes and at the same time stay focused on what's positive—every single day."

***

Later that night after Larry and Janice had climbed into bed, they reflected on the evening.

"I was so shocked to see Phil using a walker when I opened the door," Janice said.

"What surprised me," said Larry, "is that Phil, who is usually so enthusiastic and positive, wound up being like anybody else when he was suddenly confronted with a physical limitation."

"Yeah, that was interesting," said Janice. "I was so impressed by how open and honest they both were about the ups and downs they've been through. I admire that, because you know what? Anything could happen to any of us, anytime."

"Phil's a great role model," said Larry. "He really drove home the point that it's up to us to determine how to deal with a setback. I'm so glad he's decided he's not going to allow this to take over his life."

"And I like what Kelly said about refiring not just being for those who are physically strong. I have a sense that Phil and Kelly may be the most successful refirers of all."

***

One morning Larry stepped on his scale and saw that he was halfway to his goal of losing twenty pounds.

"Time to go see Dr. Jeffrey!" he said to Janice. "I want to brag a little."

On their way to Dr. Jeffrey's office, Janice commented, "After seeing Phil's struggle to recover from his back injury, I feel so grateful we've been able to refire physically over the past few months."

"That's for sure," said Larry. "I'm not going to take it for granted that I can pop into the Y and do a few sets of leg presses and bicep curls."

When they settled into their seats in Dr. Jeffrey's office, Larry and Janice were excited to share with him their Refiring Physically Code of Conduct:

REFIRING PHYSICALLY

- **Be healthy ...** Honor and strengthen your body
- **Be an exerciser ...** Move your body
- **Be a smart eater ...** Eat less and enjoy more
- **Be energetic ...** Play hard; rest well
- **Stay flexible ...** Stretch everyday
- **Learn balance ...** Practice standing on one foot

After Dr. Jeffrey looked up with an approving smile, Larry and Janice grew animated as they shared not only what they'd been doing to refire physically, but also what they'd learned about dealing with setbacks. Larry even showed off his improved pecs.

"I thought these chest muscles were gone for good," Larry said with a laugh. "Dr. Frederick praised me for the progress I've made and said my numbers are getting better and better. Guess it just goes to show that you can get back on the horse, even after falling off."

Janice gave Dr. Jeffrey a demonstration of how she could stay balanced on one foot at a time for almost a minute.

"We're starting to feel like new people," said Janice. "A friend of ours had a debilitating back injury this year, which has made us especially aware of how lucky we are to even be able to use the gym."

"Now that's a winning attitude," said Dr. Jeffrey.

PAUSE, REFLECT, TAKE ACTION

- Identify a setback—physical, financial, emotional—that you've gone through. How did you react?
- What did you learn that can help you more effectively deal with any future setbacks?
- What setback or challenge are you currently dealing with?
- What are the things you can do to address this setback or challenge?
- Choose one thing you can do and start this week.

The Fourth Key

Refiring Spiritually

9

The Big Picture

Dr. Jeffrey sat back in his chair, a thoughtful look on his face. "When I think about when you first came to see me nine months ago, I'm amazed by all the changes you've made. Talk about approaching life with enthusiasm and adding zest! You're living examples of what it means to refire. You not only think about these things—you've actually changed your behavior. Documenting your experiences has added tremendously to my research. In the emotional, intellectual, and physical areas, you're doing great."

"So we've arrived!" said Larry.

"Not quite yet," Dr. Jeffrey said. "In many ways, the most interesting and perhaps most challenging part of the journey is ahead."

"You mean the spiritual stuff," said Janice.

"Yes," said Dr. Jeffrey. "Refiring spiritually adds another level of excitement and joy to your journey. But spirituality is often the toughest conversation to have. Even tougher than talking about sex."

"I guess if we can talk about sex, we can talk about spirituality," said Janice. "But why do you think it's so difficult?"

"Because people often associate spirituality with religion," said Dr. Jeffrey, "and unfortunately, they want to be right about their religion. Unless you've both been raised with the same beliefs, it gets a little ticklish. Tell me about your spiritual backgrounds."

Larry jumped in. "We've led a pretty good spiritual life, generally. Janice comes with me to church when I ask. Our kids went to Sunday school and were confirmed, so that's been good."

"To be honest, Larry, I've been doing all those things because you wanted me to do them."

Larry turned to his wife with a look of surprise. "What do you mean, because I wanted you to do them?"

"You were raised in a fairly traditional way," Janice explained. "Your mom and dad were married forever, they shared the same faith, and you and your brothers were brought up attending Sunday school and services."

"Yes, that's right," said Larry. "And I know that your background was different."

"Different!" replied Janice. "How much more different could it be? Remember, my mother had been married before she met my father. She was an agnostic at best and he was a nonreligious Jew, so I was raised with some degree of spiritual confusion."

"Spiritual confusion—what do you mean by that?" asked Dr. Jeffrey.

"I got mixed messages," said Janice. "Mom and Dad seemed to think faith was a good thing, but they never went to temple or talked about religion. As a result, I never knew who I was, in terms of my spirituality. So, when I met Larry and he was very clear on what his beliefs were, I figured I would just go along."

"Just go along?" said Larry. "I never knew that."

"I didn't want to make it an issue. It was important to you then—"

"And it's still important to me," said Larry.

"Right," said Janice. "So I went along and it was okay. Both for me and for the kids."

"Where are your kids with their spirituality?" asked Dr. Jeffrey.

"I don't know where the kids are at this point," said Larry with a rueful smile.

"Somewhere along the continuum between faith and agnosticism," Janice offered.

"You mean somewhere between the two of you," said Dr. Jeffrey with a smile.

"Yeah, I guess that's right," said Larry.

"So given what you've been telling me, are you ready to explore spirituality now?" asked Dr. Jeffrey.

"I am," said Larry. "Since my brother Kevin died, I've been thinking about it a lot. I have a number of questions."

"I'm ready, too," said Janice, "particularly since last week, when I had an epiphany."

"An epiphany?" Larry said, laughing.

"I know it's a fancy-schmancy word, but yes, I had an epiphany."

"About what?" asked Larry.

"Remember a couple of weeks ago when I was so stressed?"

"Yeah," said Larry. "You were dealing with staffing issues at work, right?"

"Yeah. I didn't want to make a big deal about it, but I wasn't sleeping well. I was really worried."

Janice turned to Dr. Jeffrey and explained, "The person who filled my old role wasn't comfortable taking on the administrative chores. Then another opportunity came up for him and he left our organization. There was no replacement in sight. I had to cover that job as well as fulfill my new responsibilities. I also took on the search for a qualified candidate to fill the old position."

"I remember you were working a lot of hours," said Larry. "So what was your epiphany?"

"Everything changed."

"What do you mean everything changed?" asked Dr. Jeffrey.

"On Tuesday morning, our friend Kelly invited me to lunch at the last minute. Since I needed a break and didn't have other plans, I went. Kelly brought along an old colleague of hers who had recently moved back to town and was looking for—get this—an administrative position in an organization that was making a difference."

"Sounds promising," said Dr. Jeffrey.

"This woman and I really hit it off," Janice continued. "Plus, she had skills and experience our organization desperately needed."

"So that was good news, right?" asked Larry.

"Yes," responded Janice. "It was good news, but you know what? I had absolutely nothing to do with it."

"What do you mean?" asked Larry. "You were worrying about it."

"Yes, but my worrying didn't resolve the issue. Things just happened."

"Yeah, I can see how it would seem that way," Larry said, looking to Dr. Jeffrey.

"No," said Janice, "it didn't seem that way. It *was* that way. The perfect person for the job just happened to come along. Suddenly I remembered what I'd been saying to my friends over the years but never really heard myself."

"What was that?" asked Dr. Jeffrey.

"Man plans and—"

"God laughs," Larry interjected. "I've always loved that saying."

"For the first time I really understand what that means. Seeing how that issue was resolved helped me look at things in a new way," said Janice.

"In what way?" asked Dr. Jeffrey.

"Until my epiphany, I thought that every time I succeeded it was because of something I'd done."

"And?" Dr. Jeffrey prodded.

"And that's not true. While I did well in college, the fact is that I got in almost by accident."

"Really?" asked Larry with a look of astonishment.

"Yes. I guess I never told you before, but the reason I got into Beckman College is because they needed an oboe player for the band. It had almost nothing to do with me. I was not a good student in high school, but I applied anyway and got in because I played the oboe. Once I got there, I did well—and that did have something to do with me. But getting in was really almost an accident."

"That's interesting," said Larry.

"That's not all I realized," said Janice. "Looking at the downside, whenever things have gone wrong in the past, I've felt that it was my fault."

"And it's not?" said Larry with a smile. He turned to Dr. Jeffrey and said, "Just teasing."

Janice smiled. "No, it's not," she said. "Our savings and investments decreased significantly a few years ago, but that wasn't my fault—that was due to the downturn of the economy. My epiphany was that I'm not totally responsible for things going well, nor am I totally at fault when things go wrong. Something's going on that's greater than what I can control. Maybe that's what spirituality is all about, but I'm not sure."

"That's fascinating," said Dr. Jeffrey. "So that epiphany has really prepared you to talk about refiring spiritually, right, Janice? And your brother's death has you thinking about it, right, Larry?"

"Yes," said Larry. "For one thing, I've been wondering if you have to be religious to be spiritual."

"While I believe spirituality is certainly related to a power greater than yourself, it may or may not involve religion. To refire spiritually, your notion of God or a higher power has to be a concept you can do business with—in other words, it must be meaningful to *you.*"

"Makes sense," said Janice.

"I want you to talk to two people who can give you an idea of the different ways people can refire spiritually. The first is Bobby Bradford. After a challenging time in his life, he got into the grocery business. The second is Cynthia Strohmeyer, who's an astronomer at the observatory."

Dr. Jeffrey wrote the phone numbers on a piece of paper and handed it over. "Call Bobby and Cynthia and go see them. Their different viewpoints should give you some perspective on how wide the spectrum can be for refiring spiritually."

***

Bobby Bradford greeted Larry and Janice at the entrance to the supermarket he managed in an up-and-coming part of town. His big smile and bear hug instantly made them feel welcome. He led them through the store to an office in the back. Along the way, customers and employees greeted Bobby with smiles and hellos.

"Dr. Jeffrey is one of my favorite customers and one of the most caring human beings I know," Bobby said as the three of them settled into chairs. "We've had some great talks."

"He said you got into this business after a challenging time in your life," said Janice.

Bobby laughed. "That's a nice way to put it. I used to be chronically unemployed. I was down and out and felt the whole world was against me. I had a lot of anger inside, especially about my dad, who deserted me when I was just a kid. I was a really bitter man. Then I met John."

"Who's John?" asked Larry.

"He was the guy who took a chance on hiring me. He was the first man who ever really cared about me and showed me respect. He convinced me to let go of the rage inside and forgive my dad. 'After all,' he said, 'your dad was just an ordinary man with strengths and weaknesses, like all of us.'"

"So John was your mentor," said Larry.

"More than a mentor," Bobby replied. "He helped me make my life worth living. He said we're all part of a universe created by a God who loves us unconditionally, faults and all. John came to love me faults and all, which opened my mind to the idea that there really was a God who loved me that way. That started a spiritual journey for me that turned my life around."

Janice said, "Dr. Jeffrey believes that refiring spiritually adds another dimension to life and pulls everything together. Do you believe that?"

"I sure do," said Bobby. "No matter what path you follow, unless your spiritual side is strong, your ego will get in the way and you'll think life is all about you. The language may change from country to country and religion to religion, but the basic precept is the same. One way I think about it is EGO versus God or Spirit. EGO stands for Edging God Out."

"Edging God Out—what do you mean by that?" asked Janice.

Bobby leaned forward. "Let me put it this way. Did you ever notice in your career that your performance was better at some times than others?"

"Lately, yes," Janice replied.

"Me, too," said Larry.

"And have you noticed that people are fickle—sometimes they're with you and the next minute they're not?"

"Boy, that's the truth," Larry agreed.

"So your performance varies and people's opinion of you fluctuates. When you base your self-worth on outside influences like these, every day is like walking on eggshells, because how you feel about yourself is totally dependent on outside circumstances and other people. That's why I couldn't hold a job. As soon as I got criticized, I fell apart or blew up. And who'd want a person like that working for them?"

"You've got a point. But what does self-worth have to do with spirituality?" asked Larry.

"When you believe you are loved unconditionally by God, your self-worth does not depend on people, places, or things," said Bobby. "But if you get into your EGO—which can also stand for Everything Good is Outside—you exhaust yourself by searching for your self-worth out there somewhere."

Janice shook her head. "Bobby, I have to tell you, I'm a pretty skeptical person. But looking at you and seeing such peace and contentment in your face, it's hard for me to believe that you were ever a bitter guy. I'm envious. How did you get to this place? What steps did you take?"

Bobby laughed. "It wasn't always this way. And I still have my less-than-peaceful moments. But before I had a concept of a God who loved me, my goals were all really self-oriented. All I cared about was making money, becoming well known, and having a lot of clout."

"What's wrong with that?" asked Larry.

"Nothing's wrong with any of those things in and of themselves," said Bobby. "But my approach to them never really made me happy.

"I was always comparing myself to everybody else. I thought I had to be smarter, brighter, better-looking, more powerful—you name it. John pointed out to me that I was coming from a false sense of pride. As a result, I was obnoxious, always promoting my achievements, accomplishments, possessions, and the like."

"I get it," said Larry. "You were a jerk."

"Yeah, but I wasn't even a consistent jerk," Bobby continued. "I also had days when I was filled with self-doubt and fear. I was convinced I wasn't as bright, accomplished, creative, prosperous—whatever—as other people."

"I'll bet that was obnoxious, too," said Janice.

"I'm afraid it was," said Bobby. "Fortunately, John taught me about humility."

"Humility?" asked Larry. "I always thought humility was a sign of weakness."

"A lot of people do," said Bobby. "But John taught me that people with humility don't think less of themselves; they just think about themselves less."

"And how did that help?" asked Larry.

"By realizing I wasn't the center of the universe, I could focus on other people. And you know what? That brought me joy. Not to mention that it made me a lot more fun to work with and be around."

"So I get the part about false pride and self-doubt or fear causing problems," said Larry, "and that having a belief in God really helps with that. But sometimes it seems like God is so remote and out of reach."

"A lot of people have that feeling," said Bobby. "The way I brought God closer in my life was to open up a dialogue. I basically said, 'If You're out there, I need to hear from You.'"

"And did He answer?" asked Janice, arching an eyebrow.

"I didn't hear a booming voice from the parted clouds," said Bobby with a laugh. "But I felt a change in my heart. And my life began to change. I saw things in a new way—people were human beings just like me, not allies or enemies. Plus, at certain moments—enjoying the beauty of nature or reading scripture—I could sense the presence of God."

"Does spirituality always have to include God?" asked Janice.

"You can call it whatever you want," said Bobby. "In Alcoholics Anonymous they call it a Higher Power. The point is, it's something bigger than you."

"Would you call yourself religious?" asked Larry.

"Not necessarily," said Bobby. "The problem with religions—as Dr. Jeffrey and I once talked about—is that when people get involved in one, they often want to be right. If I had a magic wand and I was going to make one change in the world, I would have people give up being right. Because for you to be right, somebody else has to be wrong. And most of the wars, conflicts, and arguments around the world are win-lose battles around being right, particularly about religion."

"That's for sure," said Janice. "It's one of the reasons I've more or less steered clear of religion."

Bobby nodded. "For me, spirituality isn't about making other people wrong; it's about loving them. And it's more than a Saturday or Sunday activity. I read scripture and invite God into my life every day, which gives me a moral compass. It helps me keep my ego in check and guides how I interact with others."

"So what I hear you saying," said Larry, "is that for you, spirituality is about reaching out to God on a day-today basis for help to be the best human being you possibly can be."

"You've got it," said Bobby.

"Apparently that's really working for you," said Janice. "I love the energy in this store. Your customers and the people who work here really seem to love you."

"That's because I love them—and I love serving them," said Bobby. "I think we finally become adults when we realize that we're here to serve, not to be served. We're here to give, not to get."

"I remember Dr. Jeffrey mentioning service as one of the three ways to refire and move from success to significance," said Larry.

"It's true," said Bobby. "When you have that attitude—as John used to tell me—you'll be amazed at what comes back. He told me never to do good for other people with the idea that I'd get something back, but that if I focused on others, I should watch out, because I'd be amazed at the good that would come back to me. I know I get more out of this work than the people I'm helping do."

Larry and Janice stood up and gave Bobby a hug.

"Thank you," said Janice. "You've really shed some light on this spirituality thing for us."

10

Another Perspective

Rounding a curve on the winding mountain road, Larry and Janice saw the pale gray dome of the observatory come into view.

"Wow, what a great place to work," Janice said. "It's beautiful up here."

"I must say, I've never met an astronomer before," said Larry. "This ought to be interesting."

Cynthia Strohmeyer was certainly not what either Janice or Larry had been expecting. The red-headed woman who greeted them was in her early forties at most. Wearing comfortable clothes, she met them at the entrance to the spacious room that housed the massive telescope.

"Welcome," she said after they'd made introductions. "My uncle has told me so many good things about you guys."

"Your uncle?" said Larry, puzzled. "Oh!" he said, the light going on. "You must be Dr. Jeffrey's niece."

"He didn't tell you?" she said with a laugh.

"No," said Janice. "He just said you'd give us a fresh perspective on what it means to refire spiritually."

Cynthia led them to some seats at the edge of the gallery, where they had a clear view of the telescope. "I've been interested in math and science since grade school," she said. "By the time I reached grad school in my twenties, I identified myself as an agnostic. I just didn't find religion and spirituality compelling. Making assumptions without empirical evidence seemed so irrational to me. People who talked about God's love and miracles sounded naïve and sentimental, if not downright delusional."

"I hear you," said Janice.

"So you think people who believe in God are delusional?" asked Larry, a little defensively.

"Not at this point," said Cynthia. "I have a broader concept of what the term *God* might mean these days."

She nodded toward the telescope. "I was part of a team here attempting to take photographs of exoplanets—planets outside our solar system. Looking through that telescope one night, I had what I guess you'd call a spiritual experience."

"An epiphany?" offered Janice.

"Yes, an epiphany. Billions of years ago the universe was just a swirl of elementary particles, and now it's a place where we can build telescopes to peer so far into space that we're witnessing events that happened hundreds of millions of years ago."

"Whoa," said Larry.

"But what was the epiphany?" asked Janice, leaning forward in her seat.

"When I looked through that telescope, it suddenly dawned on me that the most complex physical structure known to man was just six inches away from the eyepiece of the telescope. That ball of elementary particles from billions of years ago had eventually resulted in the human brain—my consciousness! I just couldn't rationally believe that this was a random coincidence. There had to be a Higher Intelligence at work."

Janice nodded. "When I was a kid I had an aunt who used to say that not believing in God made as much sense as believing that the unabridged dictionary was the result of an explosion in a print shop. That never made sense to me until just now."

"How has your epiphany changed your life, Cynthia?" asked Larry.

"These days I don't simply approach my work or life as a problem to be solved. I have a sense of awe and wonder that I didn't have before. I understand that I'm relatively insignificant, but at the same time I have this sense that my life matters a great deal."

"Do you believe in God?" Larry asked.

Cynthia paused before answering. "I believe in a divine order—a Higher Mind, if you will. While that differs from the personal God a lot of people worship, it's meaningful to me.

"Plus," she added with a smile, "I know my understanding is limited. I guess you could say I'm evolving."

***

As Larry and Janice drove back down the mountain, Janice said, "Talking with Bobby and Cynthia really has given me food for thought. I can finally see why Dr. Jeffrey thinks spirituality is important in getting the most out of life."

Larry nodded. "Now the question is: how are we going to put what we've learned into action?"

"We could start by coming up with a Refiring Spiritually Code of Conduct," Janice offered.

The two of them exchanged ideas throughout the ride home, refining their ideas about what spirituality might look like in terms of a person's attitude and behavior. As they talked, Janice entered their thoughts into her tablet. When they'd settled on the main ideas, Janice read aloud:

REFIRING SPIRITUALLY

- **Be aware ...** See the big picture
- **Be forgiving ...** Give up being right
- **Be grateful ...** Count your blessings

- **Be accepting ...** Realize you're not in total control
- **Be humble ...** Realize you're not the center of the universe

"That sounds about right," said Larry. "But I'll bet it's easier said than done."

"I guess we won't know until we start trying, will we?" said Janice with a laugh.

PAUSE, REFLECT, TAKE ACTION

- How were you raised in terms of religion or spirituality?
- What events or experiences have shaped your belief system?
- The next time you compare yourself to others, stop and notice what you're doing.
- What things can you do to cultivate a sense of inner peace?
- Have a talk about spirituality with a person you trust.

Putting It All Together

11

The Refiring Gang

In time, the Last-Minute Gang evolved into a Refiring Gang—a group devoted to supporting each other in approaching life with gusto, energy, and zest.

Instead of getting together at their house for the midsummer meeting of the gang, Larry and Janice encouraged their friends to participate in a walk-run 5K to stop diabetes in its tracks, followed by a potluck in the park. To their delight, everyone cleared their calendars for the event.

"Seen any good animated films lately?" Larry asked as he caught up with his friend Rob, who was moving along at a brisk pace.

Rob and Larry were in the lead, Janice and Alice were following at a good clip, Kelly was taking up the rear, and Phil—who was no longer using a cane—would be joining them for the last mile.

"I'm watching a lot fewer movies and doing a lot more walking," said Rob, slightly out of breath. "The more I do this, the stronger I feel."

"I see the finish line and the park up ahead," said Larry. "I have to admit, I'm really ready for that potluck."

Since Larry and Rob—cheered by an enthusiastic crowd—were the first of the gang to cross the finish line, they went to the car to get the coolers. Soon their picnic table was filled with grilled chicken and vegetables, leafy greens, coleslaw, potato salad, drinks, fruit salad, and chocolate chip cookies.

"What a beautiful sight!" said Janice as she and Alice approached the picnic table. Soon everyone arrived, took their seats, and began filling their plates.

Janice stood up and cleared her throat. "Thank you all so much for coming out and supporting Larry and me in our new cause, finding a cure for diabetes. Another reason I wanted to get us all together is to find out how all of you have been doing with this refiring stuff. Who wants to start?"

"I will," said Rob. "When you two started getting into shape, it inspired me. I've made some big changes—I walk most days, for one thing. A year ago you never would have caught me doing a 5K. Now look at me."

"You look great," said Janice.

"That's not all," Rob continued. "I'm also eating differently. I grew up down South, so food was always fried and heavy on sausages, pork, and the like. I don't eat that way now—although I am going to have some of that potato salad."

"You've earned it today," said Larry.

For the next half hour, everyone chimed in and reported how they'd been refiring. Almost all of them were doing some type of exercise on a regular basis. Most were trying to eat healthier, with mixed results. Everyone said they were trying to learn something new—Phil and Kelly had signed up for classes at the local university, Rob was learning woodworking from a friend who was a master at it, and Alice had taken up the piano, an instrument she hadn't played since college. Finally, each of their friends was reassessing where they were spiritually.

Kelly was the last to speak. "This is so great being out here on a beautiful day. I'm thinking back to what our lives were like a year ago, and I have to say to our hosts, Larry and Janice—you seem so different now compared to then."

The two looked at each other and smiled.

"We are different," said Janice. "But I didn't realize it showed."

"Larry's lost a few pounds and Janice has a sassy new haircut, but it's not so much how you guys look," said Kelly. "It's just ... something about you."

"For one thing," said Larry, "I'm not working nearly as much as I used to, and Janice has taken on a major role with her nonprofit."

"But it's more than just changing roles," said Janice. "We've made fundamental changes in how we deal with life and with each other."

"That's true," said Larry. "I've stepped back from work, but I'm more engaged in life than I ever was. Working a few hours each week with young entrepreneurs at the Small Business Administration has been really inspiring and eye-opening. The business world is changing so fast that I'm learning as much from these people as they're learning from me. And remember I mentioned that I was going to be doing some writing?"

Around the table, people nodded.

"It was actually going to be a written family history, but it's morphed into a family history in pictures."

"I don't know what you mean," said Kelly.

"How many of you have hundreds, if not thousands, of pictures taken over decades stored away in boxes and drawers?" Larry asked.

Everyone said yes.

"I'm trying to figure out a way to electronically organize all these photos and bring them together into the story of our family. So I'm becoming a technology expert."

"You, a technology guru? I don't believe it," said Rob.

"My teenage grandson Paul is my senior consultant," Larry said with a laugh.

"That sounds like a good business idea—starting a company that helps people do that," said Rob.

"Maybe down the road," said Larry. "But right now I just want to get it done for us.

"And thank you, Kelly," Larry continued, "for noticing that I've lost a few pounds. The important thing is, I'm healthier than I've been since high school. You won't see me eating desserts very often, although I do intend to have a half of a chocolate chip cookie to celebrate my 5K walk today! It's not just my weight that's improved—my lab results consistently show healthy numbers. Take that, diabetes!"

There was a smattering of applause from Larry's friends.

"What about you, Janice?" asked Kelly. "What's different besides the hairstyle?"

Janice poured a second glass of sparkling water. "I always dreamed about being a risk taker, but now I'm actually acting on those dreams. And I'm finding out that with risks come not only rewards but also problems."

"You can complain to us," joked Rob.

Janice smiled. "I'm not complaining—or as my father would say, *kvetching*—I'm just saying. When I stepped into the executive director job, our organization was heading toward trouble. Donations were down and volunteers were leaving. I had to do some research, creative thinking, and networking to get us back on track. What's been surprising to me is that once I started working on these problems, I found out something I didn't know about myself: I'm pretty smart and capable!"

"We knew that," said Kelly.

"But I didn't—not really," said Janice. "This job has given me confidence in dealing with people and situations outside of work, too."

"You mean like me?" asked Larry.

"Yes, frankly," said Janice. "I speak my mind more often, don't I, honey?"

"You do," said Larry. "And you know what? I love this more confident woman I'm married to. I'm feeling closer to you than ever."

"And I love this man who's hanging around the house more, making at least a couple of dinners each week," said Janice. "Not that everything's perfect. We're learning to negotiate decision making."

"Good luck with that," Phil quipped.

"What are you negotiating about?" asked Rob, motioning for Janice to pass the chicken.

Janice handed the platter down to Rob. "Because Larry used to bring home most of the income, I used to let him take the lead on deciding how the money should be spent. Now our roles are reversed and I'm getting more involved in our finances."

"Uh-oh," said Rob ominously. "Party's over, Larry."

Larry laughed. "It's not all that bad. We're figuring it out. It's actually kind of stimulating. We'd been in the same roles doing the same things for so many years that we'd sort of stopped listening to each other."

"It's true," said Janice. "I'd forgotten what a great sense of humor Larry has."

"That's what's different!" said Kelly, her eyes lighting up. "You haven't just changed your looks and the things you're doing—your whole relationship has changed."

"I can't speak for Janice, but I know I'm changing on the inside, too," said Larry. "I'd gotten into a rut with church, attending services more out of habit than genuine interest. I decided to refire there, too. For years I'd thought about how I might put my faith into action. This year I didn't just think about it—I started a small group that brings meals and entertainment to homebound seniors. I thought it would be depressing, but it's just the opposite. I love these people—it's often the highlight of my week."

"And I finally get why Larry's church is important to him," said Janice. "I can see the peace and sense of calm it gives him. I'm also looking for that inner peace. While I don't really experience that in Larry's church, I did stumble upon something like it in a yoga class I started taking. They have several minutes of silent meditation at the end of class. Without all the words—which always sound like dogma to me—I'm able to go within and feel peaceful."

"Sounds like you two have gotten real with each other about where you are with the whole spiritual thing," said Rob.

"We have," said Larry. "These days we're much more honest with each other. Not just tolerant, but also accepting of where each of us is on our spiritual journey."

The last of the meal had been eaten and everyone began gathering up their plates.

Alice stood up and stretched. "Oh, man! The only journey I'm ready to take right now is home to a hot bath. I'm going to sleep well tonight!"

With that, the group loaded what was left of the meal into the coolers. They set a date for their next meeting, exchanged hugs all around, and headed to their cars.

PAUSE, REFLECT, TAKE ACTION

- How ready are you to begin your own refiring journey? What can you do to get ready?
- When will you begin this journey?
- Who can support you on your journey and be part of your own Refiring Gang?
- Name three things you can do to get started.
- Choose one and just do it!

12

Sharing the Experience

Dr. Jeffrey stood on the stage at the performing arts center, where he had just presented the results of his research on new models of aging to several hundred people. Near the front row, a camera captured his talk, which would be broadcast to a local television network and a wide Internet audience.

"To summarize," Dr. Jeffrey said, "what I call *refire* is not simply to stop or start working, or take a class, or to finally lose that twenty pounds. It's an ongoing process of approaching things with gusto, taking risks, and bringing enthusiasm and zest to every area of your life."

The video screen behind him went dark and Dr. Jeffrey stepped to the edge of the stage.

"Now, for those of you who've heard the statistics from my research, watched my PowerPoint, and haven't yet fallen asleep, I have a real treat for you. I'm going to bring out a couple who have lived all the things I've just talked about. We're going to hear now from Larry and Janice Sparks, who are in the midst of their own refiring journey."

Hearing their cue, Larry and Janice walked onto the stage and settled into director's chairs while Dr. Jeffrey took a seat in a chair facing them.

"Janice, why don't we begin with you?" he said.

"Sure," said Janice. "First, I'd like to thank you for inviting us here today and giving us this opportunity to share our story with such a huge audience." She took a moment to scan the crowd. "Who knew so many people would be interested in hearing what a couple of sixty-somethings have to say?"

"I'm not at all surprised at the crowd," said Dr. Jeffrey. "As I said in my lecture, you and Larry represent a huge demographic. Isn't that right, Larry?"

Larry's eyes widened and for a couple of moments he froze. Just as things were getting uncomfortable, he cleared his throat and said, "I have to be honest, speaking in front of such a big crowd makes me nervous. Now I understand why some people fear public speaking more than death."

The audience laughed, clearing away the tension.

Dr. Jeffrey said, "Okay, Larry, we'll let you off the hook for now. Janice, why don't you tell us how this all began for you."

Janice said, "A couple of years ago, we were just kind of going along on auto-pilot. Then we went to our forty-fifth high school reunion and saw how differently our peers were aging. Some were full of energy and ideas. Others looked listless and bored, and when they spoke, they weren't very interesting. We saw we had a choice about which camp we were going to be in."

"At the reunion, we ran into Dr. Jeffrey," Larry chimed in. "He told us about this research he was doing on a new, positive model of aging that he called refiring. He said he'd be happy to give us some coaching if we were interested."

"I remember that conversation," said Dr. Jeffrey. "And I was delighted when you called a few weeks later."

"Right after the reunion my twin brother died of a heart attack," said Larry. "So that was kind of a wake-up call for me. I didn't want to sleepwalk through whatever time I had left. Plus, I was stepping back from work while Janice was taking on a new job, so we both felt like it was a good time to get some direction."

"So that's how this all started," said Dr. Jeffrey. "Now tell us a little about how you've refired."

"No, we haven't refired—we're refiring," Janice corrected. "And we're still doing it—still experimenting and learning."

"Janice makes a good point," said Dr. Jeffrey. "As I mentioned earlier, refiring is an ongoing process." He turned to the audience. "Sorry, folks, you're never done."

Again, the audience laughed.

Dr. Jeffrey continued, "I'd love for you to tell us what you two did to refire your relationships."

Larry nodded and said, "We noticed we were getting kind of predictable in our social life—going to the same places at the same times with the same people and doing the same things. So we came up with this idea to start a Last-Minute Gang, where everyone agreed that unless we had a valid reason for turning down an invitation to do something, we'd do it—even at the last minute."

"And how did that energize you?" asked Dr. Jeffrey.

"It made us more spontaneous and open to new adventures," said Janice. "Not only with our friends, but also with our kids and grandkids."

"That's for sure," said Larry. "One of my best friends now is my grandson Paul, who takes me to places I'd never think to go. He'll call me up on a Saturday morning and say, 'What are you up for, Gramps?' Then we create some fun activity to do on the spot."

Dr. Jeffrey nodded. "As I said in my lecture, research shows that people who stay connected with others have better health, sleep better, and enjoy life more."

"Speaking of kids," said Janice, "as we started refiring, we found out that this wasn't just for seniors. When our adult children and their friends heard about our refiring, they got inspired to make changes in their own lives."

"Of course, not all of our refiring ideas worked out," said Larry. "I always thought it would be kind of sexy to have a motorcycle, so I went out and bought one. When I began riding it, I realized it was also pretty scary. There are a lot of big cars on the road! So apart from collecting dust, that shiny red motorcycle looks as good as new in our garage, because I never ride it."

Dr. Jeffrey laughed and said, "Those are some great stories about emotional refiring. Tell us about how you refired intellectually."

"I'll start," said Janice. "While most of my friends who had jobs were retiring, I took my volunteer work to a higher level by agreeing to be executive director at my nonprofit. At first I was almost overwhelmed with the paperwork. But then I redesigned my job so that more and more days I came home with such an adrenaline rush that it took a while to settle down and go to sleep."

"Janice makes a good point here," said Dr. Jeffrey. "You'll know you're refiring when you're experiencing what we call positive stress, which can help you achieve goals and feel alive. That kind of stress can actually be healthy—as long as it doesn't go on too long."

"Yes," said Janice. "I realized I'd taken on too much when I tried to learn Spanish on top of everything else I was doing. I got up to Lesson 5 and started getting overwhelmed. I realized I simply didn't have the time to study or practice. So I dropped that."

"So tell us about some refiring ideas that did work out," said Dr. Jeffrey.

"Sure," said Larry. "One of the big wins for me was refiring physically. When I started, I was twenty pounds overweight and a newly diagnosed diabetic. Today I'm a pretty healthy guy."

"And Larry's improved eating and exercise habits have rubbed off on me," said Janice. "I was one of those women who hated going to the gym. I still hate going to the gym. But you know what? My yoga class is my favorite part of the week."

"So what motivates you two in this area?" asked Dr. Jeffrey.

"My diabetes was the thing that pushed me into walking and eating right," said Larry, "but after a while it was how really great I felt that kept me going."

"I would have to say the same thing," said Janice. "My doctor had been encouraging me to do something about my high blood pressure, so that was part of it. But once Larry and I started eating better and I found this gentle yoga class that leaves me feeling wonderful instead of sore and sweaty, it's the feel-good aspect that keeps me going."

"Yeah," Larry jumped in. "There's this feeling you get when you're refiring. It's like you're running on all cylinders. You get addicted in a positive way to the excitement and energy you feel."

"It's true," said Janice. "One night we went to dinner with an old friend who is now living in a retirement home. All the residents were sitting around with slumped shoulders, looking like they were just waiting to die. I said to Larry, 'What if this were a refirement home instead of a retirement home? Maybe someone would stand up at the head of the table and say, 'Okay, everybody, the discussion question for the night is—'"

"So what I'm hearing," said Dr. Jeffrey, "is that once you start refiring, you build momentum."

"Sort of," said Larry. "But you have to keep at it. I did some backsliding. I realize now that it's not automatic—it's up to me whether I go forward or backward."

"Say more about that," said Dr. Jeffrey.

"It's my choice. I can either keep eating right and exercising—or I can get sick and feel crummy again. I can either keep learning and exploring—or I can get bored and depressed. I can either keep reaching out to friends and new people—or I can sit around and get lonely and grumpy. I can either keep practicing my faith—or I can start feeling like life is empty and pointless."

"Believe it or not, the spiritual thing has been my favorite part of this whole refiring journey," said Janice. "Somehow I'd managed to be married to Larry for forty years without ever admitting to him that I didn't feel at home in his church. I was afraid that telling him would put a barrier between us, but it's done the opposite."

"Why do you think that is?" asked Dr. Jeffrey.

"My husband has been so respectful of my feelings about this," said Janice. She reached over and took Larry's hand. "It's made me love him even more."

Larry shrugged. "Hey, even I don't have all the answers."

After a thoughtful pause, Dr. Jeffrey turned to the audience and said, "So to recap here, we've got two people who saw themselves getting into a rut as they grew older. Rather than letting that rut get any deeper, they refired their work, their relationship, their friendships, their health, and their spiritual lives. And don't they look great?"

The audience broke into applause.

Blushing slightly, Larry said, "Wait a minute. First of all, as Janice said earlier, we're still refiring and we get that we'll never completely arrive.

"Second, you make it sound like we're something special. We're not. We're ordinary people." He looked out at the audience. "Every one of you can do the same things we're doing. And I hope you do, because this refiring stuff is a kick in the pants."

The audience laughed.

As the laughter died down, Dr. Jeffrey stood and walked to the edge of the stage.

"You've heard me talk about refiring, you've seen the results of my research, and you've heard the impact it's had on Larry and Janice. What I'd like you to do now is quiet yourself and answer three questions.

> "**Question 1:** What have you heard here today?" Dr. Jeffrey paused to let the question sink in.
> "**Question 2:** What does it mean to you?
> "**Question 3:** How can you begin your own refiring journey?

"Now I want you to turn to the person sitting next to you and share the answers to those questions with one another."

Soon the auditorium was filled with the roar of conversation and laughter. After a few minutes, Dr. Jeffrey raised his hand to quiet the room.

"From the energy and volume of the last few minutes, it sounds like you've really got it.

"Thank you for your time today. Before I close, I want you to do four things. First, keep thinking about what you've heard today about refiring. Second, keep thinking about what it means to you. Third, keep thinking about what you can do to refire. And I'm going to put the fourth and last thing up on the screen, because it's really important."

Dr. Jeffrey hit his remote and three words appeared on the screen:

HELP OTHERS REFIRE

Acknowledgments

Over the years Ken and Morton have learned from and been influenced by many individuals. Together they thank and acknowledge

Steve Piersanti, our wise and wonderful publisher, for his vision and enthusiasm throughout the project; and

Martha Lawrence, a gifted editor and author in her own right, for her substantial contributions to this book.

In particular, Ken wants to acknowledge and thank the following people:

Jimmy Blanchard for what he taught us about bringing 1 Corinthians 13 alive as we look at how to enhance our special relationships;

Richard Bowles for teaching us that we all can make the world a better place every day by the moment-to-moment decisions we make as we interact with other human beings;

Bob Buford for what he taught us about the movement from success to significance;

Henry Drummond for what he taught us about the damage anger does to loving relationships;

Phil Hodges, Phyllis Hendry, and the **Lead Like Jesus** ministry for teaching us how the human ego Edges God Out and the importance of integrating our heart, head, body, and soul;

Raz Ingrasci and **The Hoffman Process** staff for what they taught us about the interaction among your emotional, physical, intellectual, and spiritual selves;

Tim Kearin and **Dee Edington** for what they taught us about all aspects of health;

Tim Keller for what he taught us about loving people even when they are unlovable;

Robert Laidlaw for teaching us about believing in God;

Peter Lovenheim for teaching us how to reach out to neighbors in creative ways, so we can get to know each other better;

Robert S. McGee for teaching us about the ego problems that result when your self-worth depends on your performance plus the opinion of others;

Mark Miller for teaching us that growing intellectually is like oxygen to a deep-sea diver—without it you die;

John Ortberg for teaching us what's important in life and what goes "back in the box";

Norman Vincent Peale for teaching us about the power of positive thinking, as well as for pointing out that if you are not continuing to learn, you might as well lie down and let them throw the dirt on you, because you're already brain dead;

Tony Robbins for teaching us how to develop a code of conduct;

Pastor Ryan Ross and the men's group at the Rancho Bernardo Community Presbyterian Church, for teaching us about the importance of integrating spirituality with our emotional, intellectual, and physical selves;

Bob Russell for teaching us the difference between success and significance;

Vince Siciliano for his helpful and thoughtful feedback;

Fred Smith for teaching us the meaning of real joy;

Rick Tate for teaching us that Feedback Is the Breakfast of Champions;

Terry Waghorn for teaching us about having two different groups of people managing your present and creating your future;

Margie Blanchard, my amazing wife, for being the best refiring partner a guy could ever have;

My children, **Scott Blanchard** and **Debbie Blanchard,** for keeping me young at heart.

And Morton wants to acknowledge and thank the following people:

Amy Ahfeld, a newly minted, young psychologist who contributed significantly to my earlier writings in geriatric psychology;

Laura Carstensen for her creative thinking and writing that helps us all see aging as an opportunity;

Jo Linder Crowe and the California Psychological Association for providing a forum for my writings and presentations in the area of geriatric psychology;

Debbie Graves for patiently and persistently staying with the many twists and turns between concept and completion while working on this manuscript;

Dilip Jeste for his seminal work in successful aging that has influenced my thinking and the thinking of many others;

Spencer Johnson, internationally acclaimed bestselling author, for decades of friendship, camaraderie, insight, and support;

Natasha Josefowitz, poet, author of more than twenty books, and friend, for being the best example I know of how someone can begin to refire at age eighty-plus;

Stan Pappelbaum, physician and friend, for providing me with wise counsel during difficult times and a living example of how to age enthusiastically;

Peter Sacks, my physician, longtime friend, and colleague, for having shared and been a part of so many personal and professional milestones;

Susan and Stephen Schutz, friends, colleagues, authors, and philanthropists, for showing the world the importance of caring relationships through their books, films, and cards;

Alan Sorkin, a valued friend, for exemplifying what it means to give back by his work in the nonprofit world;

The Learning Network, an extraordinary group of women and men—each of whom is committed to making the world a better place—for enthusiastically endorsing an early version of this project;

My children, their spouses, and **my grandchildren** for keeping me grounded and always coming through before being asked;

My wife, **Marjorie Hansen Shaevitz,** for being my loving, caring, constant companion, colleague, and support system.

About the Authors

KEN BLANCHARD

Few people have made a more positive and lasting impact on the day-to-day management of people and companies than Ken Blanchard. He is the coauthor of several bestselling books, including the blockbuster international bestseller The *One Minute Manager®* and the giant business bestsellers *Raving Fans* and *Gung Ho!* His books have combined sales of more than twenty million copies in forty-two languages. Ken—with his wife, Margie—is the co-founder of The Ken Blanchard Companies®, a worldwide human resource development company. He is also co-founder of Lead Like Jesus, a nonprofit organization dedicated to inspiring and equipping people to be servant leaders in the marketplace. Ken and Margie live in San Diego and work with their son Scott, his wife Madeleine, and their daughter Debbie.

MORTON SHAEVITZ

For more than three decades Morton Shaevitz has been helping individuals and organizations to grow and change through his work as a clinician, teacher, author, consultant, and speaker. As a member of the Division of Internal Medicine at Scripps Clinic, he developed a number of behavioral health programs, and his interest turned toward medical and geriatric psychology. He is currently the chair of the section of Geriatric Psychology for the California Psychological Association. He has served as a member of the Leadership Council of the Stein Institute for Research on Aging and is an Associate Clinical Professor of Psychiatry (V) at the University of California–San Diego. Morton has four adult children and four grandchildren, and he and Marjorie live in La Jolla, California.

Services Available

If you would like additional information about how to apply these concepts and approaches in your organization, or if you would like information on other services, programs, and products offered by Blanchard International and Shaevitz and Associates/MHS Consulting, please contact us at:

The Ken Blanchard Companies
World Headquarters
125 State Place
Escondido, California 92029
United States
Phone: +1-760-489-5005
E-mail: International@kenblanchard.com
Website: www.kenblanchard.com

or

Shaevitz and Associates/MHS Consulting
2671 Greentree Lane
LaJolla, California 92037
Phone: +1-858-459-0155
E-mail: Morton.Shaevitz@shaevitzandassociates.com
Website: www.ShaevitzandAssociates.com
www.MHSConsulting.com

Berrett-Koehler is an independent publisher dedicated to an ambitious mission: *connecting people and ideas to create a world that works for all.*

We believe that to truly create a better world, action is needed at all levels—individual, organizational, and societal. At the individual level, our publications help people align their lives with their values and with their aspirations for a better world. At the organizational level, our publications promote progressive leadership and management practices, socially responsible approaches to business, and humane and effective organizations. At the societal level, our publications advance social and economic justice, shared prosperity, sustainability, and new solutions to national and global issues.

A major theme of our publications is "Opening Up New Space." Berrett-Koehler titles challenge conventional thinking, introduce new ideas, and foster positive change. Their common quest is changing the underlying beliefs, mindsets, institutions, and structures that keep generating the same cycles of problems, no matter who our leaders are or what improvement programs we adopt.

We strive to practice what we preach—to operate our publishing company in line with the ideas in our books. At the core of our approach is stewardship, which we define as a deep sense of responsibility to administer the company for the benefit of all of our "stakeholder" groups: authors, customers, employees, investors, service providers, and the communities and environment around us.

We are grateful to the thousands of readers, authors, and other friends of the company who consider themselves to be part of the "BK Community." We hope that you, too, will join us in our mission.

A BK Life Book

This book is part of our BK Life series. BK Life books change people's lives. They help individuals improve their lives in ways that are beneficial for the families, organizations, communities, nations, and world in which they live and work. To find out more, visit ww w.bk-life.com.

Dear Reader,

Thank you for picking up this book and joining our worldwide community of Berrett-Koehler readers. We share ideas that bring positive change into people's lives, organizations, and society.

To welcome you, we'd like to offer you a free e-book. You can pick from among twelve of our bestselling books by entering the promotional code **BKP92E** here: http://www.bkconnection.com/welcome.

When you claim your free e-book, we'll also send you a copy of our e-newsletter, the *BK Communiqué.* Although you're free to unsubscribe, there are many benefits to sticking around. In every issue of our newsletter you'll find

- A free e-book
- Tips from famous authors
- Discounts on spotlight titles
- Hilarious insider publishing news
- A chance to win a prize for answering a riddle

Best of all, our readers tell us, "Your newsletter is the only one I actually read." So claim your gift today, and please stay in touch!

Sincerely,

Charlotte Ashlock

Steward of the BK Website

Questions? Comments? Contact me at bkcommunity@bkpub.com.

Made in the USA
Lexington, KY
07 December 2015